Pathway to the Wild

PATHWAY
TO THE WILD

by
William Condry

FABER AND FABER
3 Queen Square London

First published in 1975
by Faber and Faber Limited
3 Queen Square London WC1
Printed in Great Britain by
Latimer Trend & Company Ltd Plymouth
All rights reserved

ISBN 0 571 09934 3

'Life would stagnate if it were not for the unexplored forests. . . .
We need the tonic of wildness—to wade sometimes in marshes
where the bittern and the meadow-hen lurk . . . to smell the
whispering sedge where only some wilder and more solitary fowl
builds her nest . . .'

THOREAU

In memory of William Hubert Mappin (1891–1966) who wished his estate of Ynys-hir to remain unspoilt and to become a sanctuary for wildlife.

And in appreciation of all that has been done by his widow, Patricia, to make this possible.

Contents

🌺 Illustrations

Illustrations

Acknowledgements

The author and publishers are grateful to the following for permission to reproduce photographs in which they hold the copyright: The British Tourist Authority (Plate 3*a*), Peter Conder (Plate 12*b*), the Controller of Her Majesty's Stationery Office (Plate 14*a*, Crown Copyright), David A. Gowans (Plates 13*a*, 13*b*, 13*c*), Eric Hosking (Plates 7*a*, 7*b*, 8*b*), J. Odier (Plate 10*b*), C. P. Rose and *World of Birds* (Plate 4*c*), the Swiss National Tourist Office (Plate 4*a*).

Thanks are also due to Dr. Bryn F. Roberts of the University College of Wales, Aberystwyth, for kindly supplying the text of the Edward Lhuyd letter quoted in Chapter 1.

The author wishes to record his appreciation of the hours, the years, the lifetimes of effort and support which so many people, most of whom go unsung and unacknowledged, devote to the cause of conservation throughout the world.

1. The House by the Marsh

Winter was ending, the month was February, the day was bright, and hope as wide as the estuary skies. Penny and I climbed the stile at the edge of the wood and looked at the house across a marsh that glowed red where dead stems of cotton sedge caught the morning sun. It was an old, dark-grey house that almost seemed an outcrop from the rocky hill behind; which in effect it was, for that is how Welsh houses used to be built. People chose a site where there was water to drink and rock to build with, then they split the rock into rough slabs and up rose their new home, virtually out of the quarry it was hewn from. So, three or four hundred years ago, a little house was built, low-roofed, thick-walled, cramped. And if its construction was simple, so was its design. At one end lived the people; at the other, the cattle, with only a door to separate them. So life went on for many generations until in the mid nineteenth century came refinements. A new, taller section was added, trebling the living space; and the door between people and cattle was sealed. But they went on living close to each other, for even when we first looked into the house the room next to the kitchen bellowed as we opened the door and three young calves peered vaguely at us with big, black, short-sighted eyes.

From the house no other dwelling was visible. The view was all of a bogland edged by rushy pastures and circled by woods of oak, birch and pine. In so isolated a place it was good to find a house that still stood intact. It could so easily have been a roofless ruin or a pile of half-buried stones. For rural Wales is a land depleted of a people whose house-remains everywhere speak of a time not long ago when even the remotest, most unlikely spots were inhabited.

For several years Penny and I had enjoyed a distant acquaintanceship with this solitary old farmhouse set darkly under its oak-covered hill. Half-hidden behind a big holly it had always seemed retiring, even a little mysterious to us as we passed within a few hundred yards on our birdwatching walks to the estuary. But it was not a house we had ever thought very much about. Not until now when, suddenly, it was empty and its owner, Hubert Mappin of Ynys-hir estate, was inviting us to be its next tenants.

We came to inspect. We looked at the badly pointed exterior, the leaking roof. We looked at (and smelt) the damp wall at the back of the very dark kitchen. (Like so many Welsh country houses it was built into the hill with earth up to the eaves all along the back.) We looked at the cellar with its six inches of water in the bottom. (What optimist had thought a cellar a good idea for a house with its toes in a marsh?) We looked at the sorry vegetable patch outside the living-room window. We looked at the drinking water supply, a square, walled hole in the ground and to all appearances admirably placed to receive the drainage from the adjacent cattle yard. We looked at the long, narrow, winding, pot-holed, muddy road from the village and thought of our car springs. We looked at the mucky farmyard and the presumably rat-infested buildings.

Then we looked again at the tawny peat bog, so colourful in the morning sunlight. We were caught by this grey old farmhouse and its place in the world—its peace, its seclusion, its prospects of marsh and wood and distant hills, its nearness to estuary and sea. Yet such are the quirks of human motivation that I daresay what finally decided us to take the house was the pair of ravens who left us in no doubt that they included it in their territory. We both felt a liking for these long-winged, all-black, splendidly croaking birds which, not far from the house, were putting together a huge nest high in a group of pines that have stood long years in the estuary gales. That morning a surging easterly filled the boughs and the ravens found it difficult to airlift their sticks. Occasionally a squall sent them twirling like leaves about the sky and we heard music in their wings as they fought back to the trees. Seeing us they called deeply, resonantly, warning each other. Then they barked in anger and let the gale toss them away to a near-by hillock where they set about hacking chunks out of the

sward with their axe-like beaks. Thus frustrated ravens give outlet
to their emotions. In a few minutes they rose and circled low
above us, shouting their distaste. Over they came, bold, powerful,
almost menacing shapes against the white clouds, their wings
quickly winnowing, their nape feathers all puffed out in threat
display. Good birds to have as neighbours, we decided: symbols
of the wild and of the outcast, of those who live outside the stock-
ade and are persecuted by a world with its values all wrong. For
ravens, once universally common, have been widely exterminated.
Today in most of England, much of the continent of Europe, they
exist only as prisoners in zoos. Or they live mutilated so they
cannot fly, like those wretched ravens kept pinioned at the
Tower of London to perpetuate a mindless tradition. But in
Wales the raven is only locally persecuted and in most districts
is still splendidly abundant.

So for a touch of wildness and the company of ravens we
came to live in the house by the marsh. Its name, Ynys Edwin,
means Edwin's Island, the 'island' being a memory of far-off days
when a vast morass called Cors Fochno stretched all across this
coastal tract. But the desolation of swamps and peat bogs, not all
of which have yet been reclaimed, was never a flat monotony.
Always it has been enlivened by shapely little hills that outcrop
everywhere, hills that mostly include the word *ynys* in their names.
And maybe ever since early in history these islands have been at
least sporadically inhabited, by most people from necessity but by
a few from choice: for isolation and island life must always have
had their devotees.

We had not been long at Ynys Edwin before we began to wonder
who had lived there before us. Edwin especially. Who was he?
When did he flourish, or more likely fail to flourish, on this infertile
fang of Silurian shale? We made inquiries. We asked local farmers
and shepherds, we asked poets, preachers, professors. Edwin, we
were told by one expert, was a King of Northumbria, though how
he came to be living on a rock in Ceredigion was never made clear.
Someone else said he was a Welsh prince descended from one of
the sons of Cunedda. But who at that time in Wales was not
descended from one of the sons of Cunedda? (And anyway, who

was Cunedda?) Still others told us that Edwin (or Edwyn) was probably a saint of the early Church who established a lonely cell for himself on this bog-surrounded *ynys*. Only one thing these inventions had in common: they all craftily consigned Edwin to the Dark Ages, a nice shadowy place in history where you can't check on anybody's facts.

We soon assumed (nothing has so far made us change our minds) that the real Edwin was lost for ever in the stream of time and that we were free to accept whatever explanation took our fancy. Not being amicably disposed towards the early princes of either Northumbria or Wales, who were doubtless gory brigands one and all, we opted for Edwin the Celtic saint. We easily pictured him floating up the ocean from Brittany on a green sod or in a granite trough, the way saints used to travel. A specially ordained tidal surge then swooshed him up the Dyfi estuary to do good works ever after on the rock to be known as Ynys Edwin.

No doubt an archivist, sifting diligently through the local records, could come up with some fascinating snippets about earlier inhabitants of Ynys Edwin. But I can tell you only about Hodgson and how I discovered him. I have mentioned our cellar, how it is waterlogged, forbidding, unusable. We had noticed that the walls going down its steps were pasted all over with old newspapers. But it was years before I had the curiosity one day to examine them. Torch in hand and brushing aside decades of cobwebs I found myself reading the yellow-brown pages of the *Liverpool Weekly Post* of Saturday, 13 February 1886. But not with any joy. I soon decided that the papers of that age were just as timorous and time-serving as those of today. But then I discovered a real gem. These papers had been stuck on earlier papers and by good fortune I was able to peel off a thick top layer to disclose one that was thirty-four years older. I was now face to face with pages of the *Whitehaven News* of July 1852—a significant date because it was about then that the new addition to Ynys Edwin was said to have been made. I found that this issue of the *Whitehaven News* had been sent here by post. For written on the top of its first page was: 'Hodgson, Ynys Edwin, Glandovey, Cardiganshire'. So Hodgson, I reckon, was an early, perhaps the first occupant of the newly enlarged Ynys Edwin.

18

Pretty certainly he had come here from Whitehaven and was being sent the local paper to keep him in touch with the news back home. And why should a man move from Cumbria to Cambria? That is fairly easy. At Whitehaven they mined coal, here they mined lead. And miners have always been migrants, not by choice but by the necessity of escaping local depressions, like migrant birds driven by hard weather. In the mid nineteenth century miners from all over Britain, including many from Cumberland, came to work in the booming lead industry of mid Wales. Hodgson then was perhaps a coal-miner turned lead-miner. But how long he stayed here, whether his life turned out well or was tragic I have no idea.

Our cellar-wall newspapers, though carefully studied, told us nothing else at all definite. But what are we to make of pages from the *Annandale Herald and Moffat News* of 1886 if not that after a Cumbrian we had a Scotsman in Ynys Edwin? And to me that suggests he was a gamekeeper for Ynys-hir estate. For in those days if you wanted a top-flight keeper you invariably sent to Scotland for one. It is interesting that this newspaper, like the one thirty-four years earlier, also had an address on it, not to Ynys Edwin this time but to 'MacDonald, Keeper, ——mawr, Dolwyddelan, N. Wales'. Can we assume that this MacDonald, having read it, then passed it on to his brother, also a keeper, at Ynys Edwin? It hardly matters. Meanwhile we are leaving our cellar-wall newspapers as we found them. We cherish them for what they are—a faded whisper from yesterday. One day I am sure we shall seal off that dismal cellar altogether. Then maybe it will be another century before someone again takes a torch to read those mouldering pages. I hope they are then still legible.

As Edwin's Island is only one of many we soon began to wonder about the neighbouring *ynysoedd* (for thus does the wonderful Welsh language form the plural of *ynys*). Along our southern view across the bog stretches a mile of narrow, wooded ridge called Coed Penrhyn-mawr. But since the house most intimately associated with that ridge is called Ynys-hir, we assume Ynys-hir (Long Island) to be the ancient name of that particular 'island'. The house of Ynys-hir was destined to achieve some local importance, its estate taking in a fair amount of surrounding property: John

Lloyd of Ynys-hir built the first parish church in 1623 and John
Knolls (or Knowles) of Ynys-hir was sheriff of Cardiganshire in
1698. And doubtless the place was the seat of gentry throughout
the next two centuries.

Even the smallest 'islands' can have their treasures. Take for
example the grassy hump (that's all it is) that heaves its rounded
shape no more than thirty feet above bog level a hundred paces or
so from Ynys Edwin. Since no one I've ever asked has been able to
give a name to this particular *ynys* I assumed it never had one. Then
one day in the National Library of Wales I was shown a 1790 map
of the Dyfi estuary which not only marked this insignificant outcrop but actually dignified it with the name Ynys Celynnen, which
means the Island of the Holly-tree. Joyful discovery, for this holly
is an old friend of ours. Crowning its little *ynys* it is part of our view
across the bog. Seeing it was actually a feature on a map, I now
looked at this holly with increased respect. I knew it was big and
old but could it really be old enough to have made a map-worthy
feature nearly two centuries ago? I took a tape to measure it and
found it girthed fourteen feet at ground-level before forking into
two massive limbs. It was a far grander holly than I had thought.

My next question about this tree was: how long do hollies live?
Can they become ancient like oaks or even yews? A difficult point
because they have seldom been allowed to show what they can do.
Their hard, ivory-white wood has always been coveted for carving
and turnery and as soon as they have reached any thickness they
have nearly all been taken. So a very old holly is something quite
rare in the land. Did you know, by the way, that holly is reputed to
grow to a bigger size in Britain than in any other country? So
claimed the Rev. C. A. Johns in his *British Trees*. So while others
may look to their laurels it is clear that British conservationists
should be looking to their hollies and giving them every protection. About our particular holly I conclude it is a most ancient tree.
It certainly can have changed very little since 1905 for instance.
For in that year some vandal carved the date in its smooth bark
and the figures are still quite clear. How fascinating if we could
learn this tree's full history. Did someone plant it by a late medieval
hovel to give shelter from foul weather and the devil? For hollies

have such protective virtues and often mark the sites of vanished dwellings.

From time to time, wandering through our local woods and fields, I have found traces of former habitations, their sites hinted at by faint banks that still outline their tiny gardens; by squared stones or roofing slates sticking up through the leaf-mould; by old fruit trees or hollies; or by beds of cockleshells. For the estuary shellfish were a source of protein for people who lived off the land. Their chief fuel was peat. Summer after summer they cut away at it along systematic strips which today, though long over-grown with vegetation and invisible at ground-level, can still be clearly seen on aerial photographs. A virgin peat bog (there are very few surviving, as for instance at the National Nature Reserves at Borth and Tregaron) is raised slightly higher in the centre than round the margins. But an exploited bog has the opposite profile. It is saucer shaped and often covered with the fragrant bog myrtle, tall reeds or other elegant plants. Willows and birches may invade in due succession and an attractive, sweet-smelling, life-rich frag-ment of wilderness develops. The sort of place that should become a nature reserve. The sort of place where the local authority is quite likely to dump its rubbish unless conservationists are on their toes.

The next *ynys* past the Island of the Holly-tree is one we often walk to for its views of marsh and estuary. Especially in winter, which is hen-harrier time. Then there are always two or three of these fine hawks in the district; and since they spend more time on the wing than most raptors we often see them, the male grey-white, the female dark-brown, floating along a few feet above the surface of the bog. Is any other large bird so weightless in its flight, so full of grace and beauty? Yet harriers are shot down for fun in some Mediterranean countries and will go on being so treated until the nature conservation movement, now gathering strength in north Europe, spreads its ideas into the south.

This look-out for harriers, a long, low gorsy ridge, is Meurig's Island, in Welsh Ynys Feurig (Welsh makes curious changes in the first letter of many words). As would-be historians we were no more successful over tracing Meurig than we were with Edwin. He could be any of the broken-spirited victims of misfortune who down the ages may have struggled to survive on that bleak outcrop. No house, no living memory of a house survives. Yet old maps remember one and indicate its place. So one day I took a spade and went and searched, and found a low straight bank under whose shallow turf my blade soon rang against a line of laid stones—the foundations of Meurig's house. How I wish we could resurrect this Meurig. What a different estuary he could tell us about from the one we know today. In his time the high spring tides must have washed all round his *ynys*, bringing wigeon under his windows (assuming he had any). But now the waters are held tamely back beyond the railway bank. The fields are drained. And where was poetry is now plain dullness.

From Ynys Feurig, if we put on gumboots and feel our ankles strong enough to do battle with tussocky moor grass, we can cross first a wet field, then acres of unreclaimed bogland to a hill called Ynys Fach (Little Island) though it is in fact one of the largest islands in all Cors Fochno. (But who shall explain the endless vagaries of place-names?) On Ynys Fach I can find a couple of houses or their traces. There is Ynys Fechan, probably abandoned before 1850 and now almost gone. And there is Ynys Fach which was lived in till just before 1914, since when it has decayed gently to an owl-haunted ruin. In its day, despite the inconveniences which caused it to be deserted at last, it must have been a lovely place to live in, so quietly and sensitively is it poised on a hillside that looks across bogs and woods and away up the long slopes that lead you to the heights of Plynlimon. Two brothers still living in the parish remember their boyhood there with a nostalgia I understand.

Then there is Ynys Greigiog which has had a happier history: being nearer to the main road it has remained in occupation. Ynys Greigiog is the Rocky Island all right. The old farmhouse stands in a place of stones, its gateway two high walls where the lane has been cut with great labour through the living rock. Historically Ynys Greigiog is one of the most interesting houses round the bogland. In a region characterized by poor domestic architecture it is a welcome change to see even the modestly carved Tudor woodwork in this house. You have no need to be told that here in the seventeenth century lived someone of genteel pretensions.

22

Ynys Greigiog was built by the Pryses of Gogerddan, a family whose domain extended over much of north Ceredigion. Gogerddan House near Aberystwyth is now the headquarters of the Welsh Plant-Breeding Station. And there lived the Pryses, ruling the district like princes. And the numerous Pryse relations were scattered about in houses like Ynys Greigiog where at the beginning of the eighteenth century lived Elizabeth Pryse who is now scarcely remembered except as the writer of one or two tetchy letters (preserved in the Bodleian Library at Oxford) which she dashed off to her nephew Edward Lhuyd.

This Lhuyd is known to all Welsh people (or if not he ought to be) but, I fear, to very few English. He typified the sort of Welshman (you meet them all over the world) who is forced by circumstances to go and live outside Wales but spends the rest of his life with his birthland ever in his thoughts. A botanist when botany hardly existed (he was born in 1660, the year that saw the publication of Britain's first county plant-list—John Ray's *Flora of Cambridgeshire*), Lhuyd became a student at Oxford, then keeper of the Ashmolean Museum there. But from student days onwards he spent all the time he could in Wales, fervently gathering information about its flora, fauna, fossils, ancient monuments, folklore and language. He was a great hill-walker and probably the first man ever to know in any detail all the high ground from Snowdon to Plynlimon. Eventually he undertook to write a six-volume encyclopedia of the Celtic world, some of the information for which came from questionnaires taken round the parishes of Wales for him by Welsh students on vacation from Oxford. Possibly Lhuyd had got into the habit of recommending his friends, when they travelled in mid Wales, to go and stay with his aunt at Ynys Greigiog. So came John Angerstein, a mineralogist from Sweden, sent here in the company of Lhuyd's servant. As a consequence we find Aunt Elizabeth complaining to her nephew: 'This is the fourth Letter which I write unto you since the gentleman and your man came to Wayels into Cardiganshire . . . and you recommended them unto us . . . and wee recieved them to our howse and mayd them welcome upon your account . . . and my brother and my self sent each of us a small token being crowns a peece unto you with 2 Letters with them, and you had not the civility nor respect to write a line unto us whether you recieved them or not.'

One volume of Lhuyd's encyclopedia was to have been on natural history but he died before he could even begin it; and all his notes for it were ultimately lost in two fires, one at a London book-binder, the other at the Cardiganshire mansion of Hafod Uchdryd. So we are left sadly wondering what a man of Lhuyd's genius ('the greatest naturalist in Europe', so a contemporary described him) might have had to report about nature in Wales around the year 1700. How fascinating it would be to have even a couple of notes of his about bird-life on the Dyfi estuary or the flora of Cors Fochno, both places he certainly knew well. For when John Ray published his list of British plants in 1690 he acknowledged Lhuyd as a source of information about the flora not only of north Wales but also of the Borth district of Cardiganshire.

Forgive me if I've rather rambled on about Lhuyd but he has long been an enthusiasm of mine. There are many people revered by the Welsh, especially their hymn writers, their preachers and their politicians, with whom I have little sympathy. But with Lhuyd I feel at ease. He was attracted by so many subjects that also interest me: languages, antiquities, the Celtic past, natural history, fossils and rocks, geography and topography. Today when I go outside the garden gate at Ynys Edwin and stand at the edge of our little peat bog I like to think that three centuries ago Edward Lhuyd may well have visited this house which is only a mile and a quarter from where his aunt lived at Ynys Greigiog. If so, he probably saw and admired the same bog plants that we enjoy in our time.

What of Cors Fochno today, part of which survives so im-probably in the late twentieth century? Many have been the attempts to drain it. But though agriculture has long nibbled (and nibbles yet) around its margins, its centre, raised like the crown on a bowling green, remains inviolate, thanks to the Nature Conser-vancy Council. No doubt to some farmers and other people it is a disgraceful waste of land. But to many, including those farmers with poetry in their hearts, this great bog is a survival of a primal wilderness that is pure refreshment to the spirit when you look across it on a sunny day and see the cloud shadows playing over its zones of colourful vegetation: the warm brown of the reed beds, the white spreads of cotton sedge, the rich dark-brown of the heather, the grey-green willow swamps.

North of Cors Fochno is another still fairly intact reach of wild country, the estuary of the Dyfi, a scene that is immeasurably beautiful as the slow tides make their endless play with water, mud and light. Sometimes it is a long arm of the sea, especially when spring tides, gales and vast rains bring the flood far inland. But always in a few hours the delightful pattern of sand-banks, pools and curving creeks is re-established as the water slips seawards. How dull it would be if the tide were always in. How unbearable never again to see the ebbing of the waters, the gentle uncovering of a world that is clean washed and newly beautiful every day and is the feeding ground of all the estuary birds: curlews, godwits, greenshanks; wigeon, pintail, shelduck; and all the other colourful fowl that make up the multitudinous community of mud-flat birds. An estuary is a very special oasis. Destroy it and you rob the world of something uniquely beautiful and valuable.

So keep awake you lovers of estuaries. The philistines, be it never forgotten, are ever with us and always ready to conspire in the name of progress and economic need to blight our estuaries with dams and barrages. Such a barrage scheme has lately been suggested for the Dyfi. Nor is it the first. Over a hundred years ago someone planned an embankment straight down the middle from east to west, with the object of draining all the land to the south. So another estuary, like the one at Porthmadog, would have been ruined. If you have never been to Porthmadog you should go and see the dreadful wall a speculator called Maddocks built across the Glaslyn estuary in the early nineteenth century. If ever a wall deserved the philistines' gold medal it is this one which stretches dark, straight and hideous where once the sea waves sparkled over the bar.

Not that the Dyfi estuary has been forever untouched by industry. There was the time when smelteries stood on its banks at Glandyfi. And one of our hamlets is known to this day as Furnace. Not a title to be proud of in a countryside so full of good Welsh place-names. If we must have English words stuck incongruously on the map of Wales then Furnace ought to have hung on to its earlier, more attractive name, Silvermills. But call it what you like, this is a place with a history. Here in the seventeenth century silver and lead from all over the district were refined, the ore coming over the hills on strings of pack mules, each carrying two wicker panniers holding a hundredweight. This accounts for the existence of many an otherwise mysterious track you can still find crossing the uplands. Follow them back, these green roads, and they may bring you to the ruins of lead-mines with ringing names like Ystradeinion, Esgairmwyn, Camddwrmawr, Mynyddgorddu, Blaencwmsymlog. And if you can't pronounce them ask the nearest Welshman. For the Welsh love to sing out their poetic place-names, many of which were ancient before the first words of the Saxon tongue began to be heard anywhere in Britain.

Ore-smelting brought total disaster to our local woodlands, the primeval oak-birch cover that probably survived on these foot-hills of Plynlimon long after forests had been displaced by agriculture in more fertile regions. The records are vague but it seems that all along these mountain skirts there stretched a forest whose name was a curious mixture of Latin, French and Welsh: Boskus de Lissecoed, which might be translated as the Forest of Courtwood. (Was Hen-llys—Old Court—now a farm down the Leri valley below Talybont, the 'Lisse' in this old name?) I picture the forest breaking up pretty quickly after the medieval time when it began to disappear up the flues of the lead-mining industry. Already by 1536 we find John Leland reporting the devastation of a forest not far away. As he comes down Cwmystwyth near Devil's Bridge he notes that there 'hathe beene great digging for leade, the melting whereof hathe destroyed the wooddes that grew plentifulli thereabout'.

So likewise vanished the Boskus de Lissecoed; and so early and so completely that not even a folk memory of it seems to have survived except in a few place-names, like that of our parish: Ysgubor-y-coed, which means the Forest Barn. This was presumably a tithe barn since it was important enough to have a parish named from it. But where it stood is far from certain though some claim to know its site and to have taken stone from there for other buildings. Meanwhile the old furnace, rare in design, still stands by its much-photographed waterfall. When the silver-lead industry had done with it, the mill became in the eighteenth century a smeltery for iron, the ore coming by sea and estuary from north-west England, the fuel being charcoal as in the past. Long may it remain, this building that is such a link with the working past and which re-members the Civil War (silver from here was made into coinage for Charles I) and which saw the end of the forest of long ago.

Ysgubor-y-coed is a far-reaching, far-seeing parish, beautifully varied. Though its feet are down in the estuary tides it tilts so steeply up through woods, then brackeny slopes, that you are soon in an open land of grass, heather, rock and Bronze Age cairns at 1,500 feet. And from there you have only a few moorland miles to walk to reach the top of Plynlimon. The slopes, all of ancient rocks, have long ago been gnawed into by ice and stream to create a land of crags and diving hillsides that hang above cool, water-loud gorges green with moss and fern. For many centuries the highest lands have been sheepwalks and cattle ranges divided by old walls that flow away across the slopes and vanish over distant ridges. And in our time conifer plantations have put black forbidding crowns upon our skylines. But even spruce forests add a dimension to the scene and are interesting for the wildlife they shelter in their early stages. So I have included them too in my explorations. I have sought trees and plants, birds and mammals, reptiles and in-sects. And always there was the beauty of the place itself, the views back down the valleys to the estuary and on across the northward hills to the greater heights of Snowdonia.

There came a day when those high lands were to become much more a part of my life. It began when the famous bird-photo-grapher, Eric Hosking, came driving along the lane to Ynys Edwin in a venerable Rolls-Royce. He did not, however, come on photographic business but as an editor of Collins's New Naturalist books, bringing me an invitation to write a volume for that series to be called *The Snowdonia National Park*.

2. With a Notebook in Snowdonia

Collecting material for the book on Snowdonia was a joyous affair. Walking the wide, grassy hills; exploring up and down valleys, some with fame in the world, others folded away so neatly they are almost unknown; examining the habitats of the many animals, birds, insects, plants and trees: all this became my life for several years. I wrote as much as possible out of doors, for I wanted the reader to feel a little air on his face. I hoped, too, there would be a door at the end through which he could set off to enjoy the Snowdonia National Park in his own fashion, helped, I trusted, by having at least skipped through what I had written.

But I started indoors. I sat down and read books by former travellers because I was curious to see how the region looked to people centuries ago. It meant fighting through acres of repetition, for those old travel-writers were quite conscienceless about stealing each other's material. Much of it was poor stuff anyway. But here and there I found the odd nugget of gold that made it all worthwhile. And how cheering it was to realize that in so many of the wilder parts amazingly little has changed and that descriptions of them from as long ago as the eighteenth century are still really useful today.

Out of doors I talked with all sorts of people: farmers, shepherds, foresters, roadmen (great informers, the roadmen), quarrymen, villagers, ramblers, rock climbers, naturalists, scientists, anyone to whom Snowdonia meant something. And one man I visited was in a category of his own. This was architect Clough Williams-Ellis who, even before the Second World War, was battling for national parks in a world that hardly seemed to want them. Born in 1883, he was the son of a Welsh country squire and in due course became one himself. But squiredom in Wales was seldom the snobbish institution it was in many parts of England; and in any case Clough

Williams-Ellis cared so passionately about the quality of the environment and was so occupied with his work as an architect that there was no room in his life for the fox hunting, pheasant shooting and similar fatuous pursuits traditionally associated with being a squire. Instead he built good houses, advised on New Towns, created the exotic hotel-village of Portmeirion and worked hard to protect the Welsh environment. He was long President of the Council for the Protection of Rural Wales. A characteristic gesture was to give 300 acres of land near Snowdon to the National Trust as a nucleus for the proposed National Park that was eventually gazetted in 1951.

On a day of azure skies and sailing white clouds I went to see Clough Williams-Ellis (he was not yet knighted) at his family home, Plas Brondanw, beautifully placed in the opening of the Croesor valley near Llanfrothen. His knee-breeches tucked into bright yellow stockings, he made a colourful figure as he took me round the garden showing how in one vista he had neatly captured Snowdon between two Italian cypresses and in another the sharp peak of Cnicht. A statue of Neptune mourned the lost estuary of the Glaslyn that once glorified the view on the west until Maddocks's wall at Porthmadog blocked out the flowing tides. Though all his life he had poured execrations on what the philistines are doing to a beautiful world he spoke without bitterness. He was too cheerful a character for that, a man with a long, fulfilled career behind him. Besides, had he not helped to create a National Park with himself and his estate cocooned in the heart of it? But did I not detect his cunning hand in the fact that gay, whimsical Portmeirion was carefully excluded from the Park? Much as he loved parks and respected planners I think he was not going to risk having them breathing down his neck in the Italian-style Arcadia that he had created down there on the shore.

Plas Brondanw looks to mountains all round. Close in the west you see Moel Ddu and its neighbour Moel Hebog that in some lights are domes of purple swelling high above green woodlands. Round in the north and farther away, Snowdon rises above a landscape of naked ridges pared down by the glaciers of remote time. A little to the east Cnicht and Moelwyn are shapely crests that seem higher than their two thousand or so feet because they climb abruptly from sea-level. Scramble to any of these summits and you raise similar peaks very near and still others not far beyond them. For the secret of Snowdonia's appeal is its compactness. The narrowness, the steepness of its valleys bring the hills crowding together to produce the effect of some far greater mountain group.

It was with a light heart and a great curiosity that I set off to get more acquainted with these companionable mountains of north Wales. I began my explorations at Betws-y-coed but not because I love the place. (Who could have much affection for all those café and bed-and-breakfast notices and all that streaming traffic?) Poor Betws. 'The great Irish road to Shrewsbury runs through the village,' wrote a traveller in 1828. And so, as A5, it still does, and its impact is as crushing to the spirit as it is to the ear-drums. But Betws is a gateway to good things and it is soon behind you. Then the beauty of the vale is before you, a vale that is above all else a place of trees and the memory of a forest, the once famous Gwydir Forest which we can assume was a medieval oak land that by the eighteenth century, after much felling and replanting, was a forest where oaks now competed with beech, Spanish chestnut, larch, spruce and other introductions from the Continent. Today the bottom lands have gone largely to farming, the deciduous forest survives only as fragments, and the slopes are given up almost entirely to young conifers. But since they are conifers that here and there break the skyline by standing out on buttresses of rock their effect is acceptably alpine and very different from the depressing impact of most other conifer plantations.

From Betws-y-coed I climbed north up the conifered slopes to a plateau where little lakes with descriptive Welsh names glinted among the trees. Here for the first time in my life I heard the singing of siskins: for this spruce forest was probably the pioneer breeding place in Wales of this small, yellow-green finch formerly more or less restricted to Scotland as a nesting species. Lately it has begun to breed elsewhere in Wales and is one of the few birds to colonize the older spruce plantations. Nesting siskins usually come to our notice in April when they venture out of the forest to feed on the seeds of the earliest dandelions. This brief appearance is followed by several weeks when they lead a most secretive life in the trees, their preference being for the tallest and densest spruces where to find their nests is beyond the powers of most of us. Not till high summer do they come out of the forest again, this time bringing their young to feed on field and roadside weeds, notably thistles. But at any time of year, if you want to find siskins, it is best to learn their distinctive 'see-er' flight call.

From the siskin's world of lakelets and conifers I dipped abruptly into the valley of the Crafnant and clambered even more steeply out of it, up through many rocks and shadowy oakwoods. I squelched across one of the last remaining alder woods in Snowdonia (they have long ceased to be preserved for clog-making) and was happy to see how well the marsh hawksbeard—it has nodding, yellow dandelion flowers—was flourishing there: for outside Snowdonia this handsome plant is a real rarity in Wales. More downs and ups and I came to Pen-y-gaer, a hillfort of the Iron Age that looks east across the widening Conwy, north over fertile fields and charming woods about Ro-wen and west up the sloping grasslands that climb away to the Carneddau. Down those wide pastures a great wind came flowing from the west. And in the next few days I did much battling against that wind and its frequent rains as I clattered across the screes and botanized round the rocks and crags of Llyn Cowlyd, Cwm Eigiau and Craig y Dulyn—all delightful wild country that led me on and up to those splendid viewpoints Carnedd Dafydd, Carnedd Llywelyn, Foel-grach and Foel-fras which look across all north Wales.

Then I walked on into the west. The distant sea shone all along the north while evening darkened the ridges south to Cadair Idris. I came to Pen yr Oleu-wen that looks down 2,000 feet of ankle-challenging rocks and roughness into the deep trench of Nant Ffrancon. The great grasslands of the Carneddau were now behind me. Across the pass sharper, craggier summits rose towering and black against the westward sun.

In the next few days I explored the delights of Cwm Idwal and its lovely tarn, its high encircling cliffs and the perfect symmetry of the down-arched rocks that are cleft by Twll Du, the Devil's Kitchen. I photographed mountain avens, moss campion and the rare and minute Snowdon lily. And I met an endearing character called Evan Roberts, one of the rare ones of this world, a man who had once worked in the now abandoned slate-quarries on Moel Siabod but had become a self-taught botanist who knew more than anyone else about the alpine plants of Snowdon and sister mountains. It was good to botanize with one who was so genuinely excited by the plants he pointed to along the ledges.

Above Cwm Idwal's flowery lime-rich cliffs I came up to the twin heights of Glyder where slabs of lava lie in fascinating heaps. I followed the ridge to the rugged top of Tryfan. After the cool, moist, plant-rich crags in the corrie below, these bleak summits of hard acid rock were a botanical desert. But it was good to be up there treading the grey carpet of woolly-haired moss among the debris of yesterday's world and thinking about the slow forces that have shaped the earth, and will go on shaping it long after the trivial human incident is over.

I climbed Snowdon. It was a rather wild scramble up no recognized route because I followed the wet and slippery way of the plant-seeker. As Lhuyd wrote in about 1690: 'It's observable that on most of these high hills, ye rarest plants and the greatest variety are to be met with by ye rivulets of water that descend through the rocks from ye top of'm.' So I inched myself gently up from one dripping ledge to another and clambered across screes from one wet gully to its neighbour. 'The way I went up was directly through the rocks from Llanberrys,' said Lhuyd. That way I had come too. And now I was, as I think Lhuyd had been also, face to face with the floristic splendours of Cwm Glas. Not that it was the rarity of the plants that delighted me, for I found no real rarities. It was the unmistakable health and happiness of this whole mountain flora, composed far less of true alpines than of quite familiar lowlanders that have taken with the utmost success to the upland life. So though it was good to see holly fern and other rather élite species I got just as much pleasure from the gay throng of primroses, wood anemones, water avens, globe flowers and other fair commoners that down in the lowlands had been over for several weeks. For this is a chief joy of mountain botany, to go up there even in July and find the year still new.

The very peak of Snowdon I avoided, because I have a horror of mountains with railways up them and cafés on top. I was fully content to explore the great cirques in the mountain's flanks and all the valleys that in due course led me away to Snowdon's lesser neighbours: Siabod, whose shoulders give you an unequalled look back into the Snowdon Horseshoe; Moel Hebog, which points the way west to all the hills of Lleyn; Cnicht and Moelwyn, whose grassy steeps and rock-girt lakes I knew well from the time I lived in the delectable Nanmor valley.

From a buttress on the southern slopes of Moelwyn I looked down the sloping face of a far-spreading oakwood and thought of William George Oakley who, having made a pile of wealth out of Ffestiniog slate, returned some of it to the vale by planting the slopes with woodlands that survive today. But they survive, let us never forget, only because in the 1960s conservationists campaigned successfully to save them. Till the moment when money came flowing in to preserve these woods I doubt if anyone realized how strong is people's affection for our native trees.

In their untiring search for the 'Picturesque', romantically minded travellers of two centuries ago (and a multitude of later imitators) were all enthusiastic about the Vale of Ffestiniog. 'Nothing can exceed the beauty of this little vale,' one of them claimed in 1798. 'It is a tract about four miles in length, composed of rich meadows whose sides are edged with thick groves; and barren rugged precipices enclose the enchanted scene.' It was in the heart of this Arcadia, at the house called Tan-y-bwlch, that Oakley came to live. It was a period when prosperous landowners everywhere were building lavish mansions, laying out spacious grounds with terraces, gardens, vistas, grottoes, lakes, waterfalls and follies. They improved roads round about, reclaimed land, encouraged agriculture and, revolutionary idea, even began to spare a thought for their tenants.

They also planted millions of trees, mostly oak and beech and larch. So by the time of Oakley's sudden death in 1811 a traveller was able to describe Tan-y-bwlch as 'romantically embowered

C

with woods which occupy the steep rocks behind and wave to the breeze high above the mansion'. It is fitting that this house among the lovely woodlands (go in spring and hear the songs of all the redstarts, wood warblers and pied flycatchers) is now the head-quarters and study centre of the National Park.

Close to the dour slate town of Blaenau at the head of the Vale of Ffestiniog you see a shapely dome called Manod Mawr. An altogether beautiful mountain but for me fraught with such special obstacles that I have never managed to get quite to the top. It is the same with several of these Snowdonia peaks whose lower rocks especially are a rich mixture of sedimentaries and volcanics. They are not high these hills, they face you with not even a hint of a climbing problem. It is just that if you are anything of a naturalist they stop you at the first cliff face you come to along their lower skirts. You begin to see interesting plants bristling along the ledges or poking shyly out of crevices. Perhaps nothing more than roseroot, green spleenwort or hairy rock-cress. But these are signi-ficant plants. Choosy. They don't grow on any old rock. They whisper that you may be getting on to some good lime-rich rock and that rarer plants could lie ahead. Of course the chances are that you will find very little, that you will simply be led on in hope. And on and further on, searching patiently and quite happily at a crawling pace round the mountain's hem instead of making head-way towards the summit. So the hours pass and at the end you've probably discovered nothing of any consequence. Never mind. You've been contented in that sweet-smelling place up there in the mountain wind. And you'll get to the top next time . . .

East of Manod Mawr stretches a far-spreading moorland known as Migneint, a name that to a Welshman is soggy with the idea of quaking peat bogs. It is an upland which over the years the farmers have often tried to drain, an enterprise in which I wish them all the failure in the world. For to deprive Migneint of its quagmirishness would be to rob it of its quintessential, plover-yodelling, snipe-bleating, curlew-calling wildness. And we need our wild places more and more—and far more urgently than farmers need what can never be anything better than fifth-rate pasture, drain it how they will. But though we in our town-escaping days may love

Migneint, it aroused no admiration in earlier tourists. Thomas Pennant, for instance, describing one of its lakes, Llyn Conwy, in the eighteenth century, reckoned it 'most dismally situated among rock and bog'. Today we are grateful for lakes like Llyn Conwy and for Migneint's heart-lifting, breezy, clean spaciousness as we go across and down to Ysbyty Ifan or Penmachno.

Pennant, by the way, spoke of three islands in Llyn Conwy that were 'the haunt of the black-backed gulls during the breeding season. They are so exceedingly fierce in the defence of their young that I knew of a man who was nearly drowned in an attempt to swim to their nests, being so violently beaten by the old birds that he thought he escaped well with the dreadful bruises he received.' Disappointing to find exaggerated nonsense like this so solemnly reported by Thomas Pennant, distinguished author of *British Zoology* (1777). But it shows how easy it is for alarmist false-hoods to run riot about all predators from baby-snatching eagles to man-eating wolves and bears.

From Manod Mawr the volcanic rocks, turning south-east to lose themselves below the peats of Migneint, rise again in triple-peaked splendour on Arennig Fach, Arennig Fawr and their lesser neighbour, Llyfnant. South of them the country flows down slopes that are sometimes rocky, sometimes grassy; but all lead you at last into the long trench that is the Great Rift Valley of Wales. Africa's rift is 4,000 miles long, that of Wales less than forty: but both result from those inborn stresses that go on for ages wrinkling and splitting the surface of the earth. Africa's rift is recent and still in progress (the grumbling of its tensioned rocks is often heard and felt). But like Scotland's rift (the Great Glen) the rift of Wales is of very long ago and the rocks are now rarely disquieted. Perhaps along each side of it great cliff-faced escarpments once stood facing each other as they still do along part of the rift of Africa. If so they have vanished in the erosion of many millions of years. And in geologically recent times there have come glaciers to round the profile of the valley. Across it the melting ice left a barrage, the debris of the ancient crags, a barrage that eventually made a foundation for the Norman town of Bala which, in its street pattern, is still the town of today. The same glacial barrage also impounds

Llyn Tegid, a typical rift-valley lake, long, narrow and deep. The largest natural sheet of water in Wales, it extends for nearly four lovely miles and deserves every protection. But will it get this? So attractive a water (Tegid means beautiful) is just the place for philistines to come with their development schemes.

It was at a meeting of the West Wales Naturalists' Trust at Llyn Tegid that I first saw a gwyniad. Zoology students from Liverpool were netting these interesting fish (the only way to catch them for they take no angler's lure) and we were able to see how silvery they are and hence how they got this Welsh name gwyniad which you might translate as 'whiting' or 'white fish'. Other whitefish populations live isolated in other British and Continental lakes. Presumably at first all one species, they have by long separation grown slightly different from each other. Life is restless, fluid, malleable, always responding to new conditions. A fish cannot be sequestered in a lake for thousands of years without becoming something special in the world. So the gwyniad is now unique, a race if not a species of its own, and as such should be carefully conserved along with the shining lake that is its home.

South of Bala the country is different. You find the mountainy outlines of Arennig replaced by the long smooth shape of the high moorland called Berwyn. It is a change of scenery brought about by a change of rocks: from those of Ordovician time to those of the next era, the Silurian. On much of Berwyn's broad back the peat lies thickly blanketed and there is a mantle of heather that harbours many red grouse. And if in June you bend down and part the heather you may find that little, purple-red orchid-jewel, the lesser twayblade. But you need to know just where to look. Or have the luck of old Harry.

I had crossed Berwyn several times on foot following trackways that could easily be prehistoric. But now I walked it from end to end—from Corwen to the pass of Bwlch-y-groes. It was not a vast walk in distance. A crow would have oared himself leisurely over those twenty or so miles in less than an hour and have had time to eat a few bilberries on the way. But poor earthbound man, stumbling waist-deep in heather and sinking into pools of bog moss, makes it the labour of a day and finishes on his knees. From Cadair

Berwyn I looked round at a vast spread of Wales; up the slopes of Moel Sych I scrambled through bushes of cloudberry which in Wales is found only on Berwyn—it has showy white bramble flowers but it fruits only very shyly; and in the evening, as a reward for careless map-reading, I found myself struggling down an awkward, red-soiled erosion gully in the side of Bwlch-y-groes. From here I escaped eventually and in semi-darkness got down into the leafy valley of the upper Dyfi and reached that place of much history, Dinas Mawddwy.

The country round Dinas Mawddwy could keep you happy a long time if you have any feeling for rocks and their history; or for dramatic land forms; or for the fascinating story of man's impact on the land since ancient times; or for animals, birds, fish and wild plants. Chief sculptor of the region since the last glacier deposited its final moraine and melted away has been the fiery-tempered Dyfi river whose springs are in the grey rocks of Aran Fawddy. And there are the Dyfi's exquisite but equally tempestuous sidestreams that drop down high falls into the main valley, all hard at it carving, chiselling and hammering to produce the gullies and gorges of future time.

The Dyfi is famous for its salmon and its sea-trout. Or, sport for children turning over midstream pebbles, there are darting little bullheads and stone loaches. For naturalists with the patience to look for droppings on river-banks or under bridges there are otters to be traced, perhaps even seen or smelt. (Yes, some people can detect otters by the scent these animals leave on favourite boulders.) For birdwatchers there are dippers and wagtails at the riverside; merlins, ring ouzels and grouse up in the heather zone. 'Multitudes of red grouse and some black,' reported Thomas Pennant in 1773 in his *Tour in Wales*. 'The black game is extinct,' commented John Rhys in the 1883 edition of Pennant's book. But Rhys was a Professor of Celtic in the University of Oxford and the question must be asked: are Professors of Celtic in the University of Oxford to be trusted on the subject of black grouse on Berwyn?

If the black grouse ever did become extinct on Berwyn it is certainly back there now, and on Aran Fawddwy too, as I have reason to know, having once gone up through forestry plantations in the dark to see and hear the strange courtship display at first light. Hidden in the shadow of a big glacial boulder a party of us crouched and watched as the cold pallor of dawn slowly etched the sky with the black points of young conifers surrounding a clearing. Then startlingly loud and clear, the chuckling of a blackcock, immediately answered by another. Very soon the arena was alive with the whole crazy show of mock battle as half a dozen of the yodelling birds advanced and retreated in the stereotyped dance with which blackcock have no doubt heralded the spring dawns of untold years. This was an excursion of especially valued memory because one of our party was the nature writer and photographer Frances Pitt, then getting rather an old lady but still as energetic in the pursuit of animal studies as she had been all her life. Nor was she the only veteran lady naturalist present at our chilly dawn party: there was also Mary Richards, then a distinguished Welsh botanist of nearly seventy, yet only just embarking on what was to be the greatest period of her career as a naturalist—her many enthusiastic years of field-botany in the remotest wilds of Zambia and Tanzania.

A snippet I treasure from Pennant's remarks on Dinas Mawddwy is the hint he lets fall about a sportive use of peat paths in his day. At that time, and till well into the twentieth century, most upland farms had their sledge tracks (many are still traceable) going steeply up to the moorland where the peat was cut and dried in summer and brought down for winter burning. But listen to Pennant. He speaks of Dinas Mawddwy 'beneath the rock Craig y Ddinas whose peat paths I now survey with horror, reflecting on a frolick of my younger days in climbing to its summit to enjoy the pleasure of darting down again in one of the peat sledges'. So easy to think of Pennant as a dignified savant turning out erudite books in his study at Downing, Flintshire; so hard to picture him as a young rascal larking on the slopes of Merioneth. And it raises a couple of interesting questions. Did the mountain Welsh regularly use their peat tracks as toboggan runs? And what brought the youthful Pennant holidaying at Dinas Mawddwy which in those days was so very remote from Flintshire?

Pennant it seems (I speak now of Pennant the mature and learned traveller) climbed Cadair Idris only once in his life. It was a poor day—'so wet and misty, that I lost the enjoyment of the great view from the summit.' But he was compensated by that exciting prospect you get in bad weather up there, that of looking down on both sides of the ridge and seeing the deep, black corrie lakes far below revealed and then blotted out and then uncovered again as the clouds swirl and play round the precipices. One observation he made was rather acute for as early as 1770. He remarked that the summit was 'covered with huge fragments of discoloured rocks, very rugged, and cemented by an apparently semivitrified matter, which gives them a very vulcanic look.' After Pennant the volcanity of those rocks was doubted by many, before it was finally established by expert geologists. Fascinating also to hear Pennant talking about a road that went right over the ridge of Cadair Idris from near Llyn Gwernan to Llanfihangel-y-Pennant—'perhaps the highest road in Britain, being a common passage even for loaden horses'. Imagine anyone going that way today in the ordinary run of business!

When he had followed the track called Ffordd Ddu from Dolgellau to where it overlooks the wide, flat valley of the Dysynni, Pennant tossed up whether to go down to the coast at Tywyn or whether to go to Talyllyn. He found out later, when he had got hold of Lhuyd's manuscripts, that had he gone to Tywyn he would have seen some rare inscribed stones including the earliest surviving specimen of written Welsh (it is still there in the parish church). But not knowing this at the time he chose to turn inland where he confirmed the breeding of 'corvorants, rock pigeons and hawks' on Craig yr Aderyn (Bird Rock) but was exasperatingly vague on further details. From his description of the district it has evidently not changed much except that the ruins of Castell y Bere have been rescued from the undergrowth and there is now a main road up Talyllyn Pass. The 'beautiful lake about a mile long' with 'only a narrow road on one side' is not altered. It remains 'very picturesque' where 'it contracts gradually into the form of a river and rushes through a good stone arch into a narrow pass, having on one side the church, on the other a few cottages mixed with trees'.

Is this, then, what we need for all Snowdonia, that it shall remain unchanged from everlasting to everlasting? No, this is too much to expect in a region which, except for a few high peaks and crags, is very far from being uninhabited wilderness country. But what we should strive for is that any changes which do prove inevitable should be proceeded with as slowly and sensitively as possible. Snowdonia was made into a national park in order to protect a magnificent region from disfigurement. But this was an institution founded on loose sand because Parliament has never passed any laws safeguarding national parks from being industrialized, drowned by reservoirs, planted all over with conifers, used as military training grounds or from any other threats. The only difference between national park land and other land is that planning controls are usually assumed to be a little more strict in the parks. So we are left with the unpleasant truth that Snowdonia could be devastated by the combined impact of tourism, the electricity industry, mining, quarrying, house building, afforestation, reservoirs and main roads; and that it would all happen quite legally.

Then what hope, you may ask, for the future of Snowdonia as a national park? The answer is, I think, that there is considerable hope. And it is based on one certain fact—that a very large number of people genuinely and deeply cherish Snowdonia as one of our very finest tracts of mountain country. As the land of Britain in general becomes ever more urbanized and uninspiring, even soulless and squalid, so people are going to hold national parks and similar special areas in ever greater esteem. And eventually public opinion must compel a reluctant government to set up proper legal safeguards that will prevent all exploiters whether private or public from getting their hands on such well-loved regions as the Snowdonia National Park.

⚘ 3. A Park in the Engadine

Thinking and writing about Snowdonia made me curious to see what national parks were like in other lands. So when my sister and her husband invited us to go camping in Switzerland we were delighted. For in Switzerland, we had heard, there was a very fine national park away in the eastern mountains near the border with Italy and Austria.

On a day in July we set off from Ostend, a journey most vividly remembered for the hedgeless Belgian, then French, roadsides yellow with wild parsnip, blue with chicory and meadow sage, and pale-pink with hoary plantain, a wild flower which, though so beautiful, was condemned on public notice-boards as a pernicious weed of agriculture. (What a sad world it will be when officialdom has succeeded in exterminating all the plants and animals it happens to dislike.) The lowlands ended and the country began to build up strongly as the Vosges mountains rose in eastern France. And quite suddenly (but only for a few miles) there seemed to be red kites everywhere, either flying low over cornfields or simply walking rook-like about ploughlands picking up worms: a strange sight for us who know the kites of Wales as birds mainly of wild hills and sheep moors, and hardly ever associated with cultivations. The hunting methods of these French kites were fascinating. They flew slowly, about twenty feet above ground, searching the fields systematically; occasionally, with a quick upthrow of long wings they dropped out of sight among the crops to seize some small prey. Seldom in Wales do we see kites foraging so exactly like harriers. More often they circle rather high, then drop with arrow-like stoop.

Under wooded slopes the highway, though marked on the map as a bold scarlet streak across Europe, had narrowed to the size of an English country road. On both sides it was planted endlessly with fruit trees and these together with the telegraph wires made a perfect habitat for woodchat shrikes—the wires for perching, the trees for nesting. We watched a colourful male shrike as he gazed intently earthwards, then dropped off his wire, picked up a beetle in the grass and flew with it into a pear tree on the other side of the road, coming out immediately with his beak now empty. Crossing over to this tree we saw a little, coarsely woven nest in which, so late in the season, we expected to find well-grown young. Instead, off went the female woodchat, not flying away but planing on rigid wings in a graceful curve to the ground where she fluttered and pretended to be injured. Her nest, deeply cupped and carefully lined, held five eggs, greenish and prettily speckled.

We reached Strasbourg, crossed the broad, murky Rhine into Germany and turned immediately south along a winding road with Cotswold-like villages along it and the same gaiety of plants that had come with us for so many miles. And now there was an additional exuberance of tall vetches—deep blue, blue-white, bright pink—with masses of white melilot and scarlet poppies: they made the drab memory of some of our British roadsides, close-clipped or blasted with chemical weed-killers, something to feel ashamed of. Happy the land, we said, that is not afraid of a few wildflowers along its roads.

We entered Switzerland and came at last to Lucerne where, in the early morning, migrant willow warblers whispered sweet post-breeding songs in lakeside trees. Common and black redstarts fluttered among the leaves and, as if apologetically, a blackcap offered us a few remnants of a spring song he had already nearly forgotten. Over the water black kites squealed as they circled in endless search for floating scraps. We walked into the town to see the alpine swifts. For the curious fact is that this bird, so characteristic (in some parts of the world) of wild and remote mountain cliffs, has long-established colonies in Lucerne and other towns. Its headquarters at Lucerne are in the historic water tower that forms part of the old bridge across the Reuss where it flows out of the lake. Here scores of these large, white-bellied swifts have their nests and, as we eventually discovered, one of the best times to see them is at their evening gathering when they put on a spectacular wheeling display above the tower, not shrieking like common swifts but sending a much softer chorus down through the dusk.

Each day we were at Lucerne common swifts were passing south, their nesting quite over. But the alpine swifts were still in full courtship fervour, for their breeding season goes on until September. Then they, too, slip away over the Alps to Africa.

In a narrow street of the older part of the town I heard sweet trilling from a bird overhead. A caged canary, I supposed, that someone had hung at an upper window. But when I searched I found a row of small birds perched like sparrows along the guttering of a building, one of them strikingly yellow. Through my binoculars I could see from their streaky yellow-brown plumage that they were serins and that the very bright one, the only adult male, was producing the song. As I watched they swept down and away along the street in a tight redpoll-like flock, twittering loudly as they vanished among the leaves of a tree in one of the squares. In Lucerne I had expected to find serins in the larger gardens of the outskirts or in the quiet grounds of the crematorium above the town, not down here in streets full of traffic. As the serin is at present spreading in the continent of Europe, let us hope it is destined to bring its canary song to some of the towns of Britain also.

From Lucerne you see sharp, snowy peaks rising all along the south and you wonder, if you're new to the place, how you may most quickly find your way up to the alpine zone. We got a map and picked out a valley called Melchthal that looked as if it offered an easy route to the snow. A lucky choice, for this Melchthal soon lifted us boldly up through beechwoods, then evergreen forest, towards green mountain shoulders with crags below them and eternal snows above. Farmers were cutting or carrying hay on exceedingly steep meadows that made tongues into the hemline of the conifer forests. Perhaps the cutting of the flowers in so many meadows had concentrated the butterflies into the remainder: for those uncut were quite dancing with marbled whites, silver-washed fritillaries, large coppers and a bewilderment of blues, browns and skippers.

The sub-alpine flora, so rich in species, was especially magnificent for the massed colour of the blue milk-thistle (*Mulgedium alpinum*); the white-flowered buttercup (*Ranunculus aconitifolius*) that grows tall and elegant along wet roadside banks; and above all the masterwort (*Astrantia major*), one of the finest of all umbellifers, its pink-tinged, pale-grey sheets spreading far through the beech-woods and near-by meadows. The skirts of the conifer forest gave us burnt orchids a foot high and boggy hollows gay with spotted orchids subtly different from those we see in Britain. On dry sunny slopes we found a famous Swiss plant, the stemless thistle (*Carlina acaulis*) whose yellowish flower, three inches across, nestles almost on the ground among silvery bracts that contrast with a surround of green serrated leaves. Thoreau said a naturalist setting off for the day might take a long time getting from his door to his garden gate. Certainly a botanist in Switzerland could easily get so involved with the sub-alpine flora he might never get to the alpine zone at all.

On that first day in the Melchthal we, too, failed to reach the alpines. But what beat us mainly was the weather. Grey clouds, ragged and swirling, hung close over us all up the valley, hiding the summits of the raven-croaking, limestone cliffs. Then at mid-day the rain sluiced down and we retreated, stopping only to watch a pair of black redstarts that had a nest under the eaves of a roadside hut. They had all the timidity of the common redstarts that breed each year in the walls of Ynys Edwin or in our nest-boxes—the same studied approach, the silent slipping into a near-by tree, the quick dash into the nest, the equally furtive departure ending in a momentary splash of fiery orange as they disappeared round the corner. The hut itself was instructive. It was in fact an apiary. In snowy regions you don't keep your bees in separate hives where they would get frozen to death. You keep them all safely under one roof, say a dozen colonies to a hut, each colony having its separate entrance. Sometimes these entrances are all painted in different colours to prevent the bees from getting confused. But does it really make any difference?

Next day we went up the valley again but this time in brilliant light, every peak standing up with faultless clarity. Resisting the seductions of the sub-alpine flora we drove straight up to Stockalp, the hotel centre now almost inevitable at the head of Swiss alpine valleys. Above Stockalp we soon reached the snow, a relict patch of it filling a hollow among the boulders of an old moraine. And here, just escaping from their winter blanket, were our first soldanellas, dozens of them, hanging their fringed violet bells two or three inches above the snow. So a magic door opened for us, the door that leads into the world of the true alpine flora.

Near the soldanellas was a familiar and favourite alpine of the Welsh mountains, the starry saxifrage, quite perfect among the stones of the moraine. Its neighbour was a much taller saxifrage (*Saxifraga rotundifolia*) with large leaves and a showy panicle of purple-spotted, white flowers. *Gentiana verna* also grew here, a spring beauty of the lowlands but which flowers all summer near the snow. There were bright-pink cushions of *Erinus alpinus*; carpets of leaves of mountain avens with a very few flowers still lingering; frog orchids much taller than ours in Wales; plenty of very fine specimens of the small white orchid; and alpine butterwort which is like a smaller version of our common butterwort, with flowers not violet but cream spotted with yellow. Giants among all these fairies stood the brilliant orange-yellow daisy, *Arnica montana*; a two-foot-high gentian (*Gentiana purpurea*) whose clusters of red-brown heads were just showing colour; the common dock called monk's rhubarb which covered the ground like cabbages; and a distinguished-looking plant with strongly veined, oval, pointed leaves and tall spikes of greenish flowers called false hellebore (*Veratrum album*), a member of the lily family, very stalwart but also very poisonous. So we went on from treasure to treasure: not always sure we were giving quite the correct names to all those primulas, gentians, buttercups, saxifrages, androsaces, sedums, potentillas, silenes and veronicas. But it was so wonderful to meet this superb flora for the first time that we were happy to postpone the labours of identification.

Botanists seldom see birds. In fact botanists can be compared with that large and well-known fly, *Rhagio scolopacea*, that comes out in spring and when it settles on a post or a tree always rests head downwards and so is called the down-looker fly. I am habitually more a bird-watcher than a plant-seeker but when I do go botanizing I, too, become a down-looker. Somehow I become oblivious of birds, I don't even hear them most of the time. So on that first day in the Alps I had to make a deliberate effort to detach my attention from the ground and look around at the trilling flocks of alpine choughs, the water pipits that rose and fell in song, the occasional snow-finch that went speeding by. But one bird we did stop to look at. We saw it dash into a crack in a rock face, we heard a churring of young being fed, then the little parent bird came bolting out of the hole and went off with rapid, level, starling-like flight. But this, whatever it might be, was no starling. So we waited. Fifteen minutes later it came back and this time we got a proper view of it—our first alpine accentor. There was much about this bird to surprise us. We knew it was a cousin of the hedge-sparrow and expected to see something rather similar. But far from it. This was a much more robust, faster-moving bird than any hedge-sparrow, a bird that swept headlong round the rocks like a ring ouzel. What was more unexpected was the richness of the plumage, as if a hedge-sparrow had been splashed with white and reddish paint all over its mantle and wings, and even more striking, its flanks were lavishly touched up with short, rust-coloured stripes. Altogether a splendid bird, worthy of its virile surroundings.

After three days we left Lucerne for the Engadine by the southward main road along the lake, camping that night in a forest at the approaches of the St. Gotthard pass. It was to the sharp 'chup-chup-chup' of crossbills that we woke early next morning. We scrambled up through a chaos of tumbled rocks till we were level with the pointed tops of the spruces and soon the restless crossbills, seven of them, came in undulating flight to settle in the nearest tree, their calls ceasing instantly they landed. One was a bright red male, the others dingy green-brown. Six of them attacked the cones slowly, methodically, wrenching the scales apart. The seventh stood solitary on the highest tip of the tree motionless, sentinel-like, outlined so sharply against the white dawn sky we could see its crossed mandibles clearly. In only a few minutes they all burst out of the tree for no apparent reason and were gone twittering across the forest.

Somewhere along the road the previous evening we had evidently left the limestone behind us. For now the rocks were of granite and the screes bright green with parsley fern. There was heather too, and bilberry, wood sage, tormentil, goldenrod and polypody fern. We might have been going up the Foxes' Path or some other scree in Snowdonia. But then we came upon a patch of yellow foxgloves and this brought us back to reality. There was also the charming, white-flowered, lesser masterwort (*Astrantia minor*); and the snowy woodrush (*Luzula nivea*) whose silver-white panicles had tempted someone to pick a bunch only to tire of them and drop them along the track. We were breaking camp when a woodcutter, axe on shoulder, passed on his way up into the forest. Soon his wife and daughter followed with baskets and began picking the thickly clustered red berries off bushes of the alpine elder. These, the woman told us, were for making a 'ver good confiture'.

At Andermatt you can choose between going straight on over the St. Gotthard and down into Italy, or turning west over the Furka pass, or east over the Oberalp. We took the east road which by astonishing curves, loops and zigzags lifted us quickly higher and higher over the village. Up there the meadows, most of them still uncut, were patched blue with campanulas and rampions and pink with the crowded flowers of bistort. But this had to be a motoring day and the only new plant I remember was a charming pink that had small deep red flowers, *Dianthus carthusianorum*. A new butterfly, which we saw when we stopped for lunch, was the apollo, a fine large creature, with wings grey and transparent, the forewings blotched with black, the hindwings with four red circles. Lifting a stone I uncovered a nest of small black ants in whose midst was a woodlouse-shaped green caterpillar that seemed perfectly at home and was presumably the larva of one of those blue butterflies that enjoy miraculous relationships with ants, supplying them with sweet secretions in return for food and lodging.

We came down the valley of the upper Rhine to Chur (the river here an alpine torrent swollen and blue-white with melt water), then up the Landquart river to Klosters, thence to Davos and over the Flüela pass and down to Zernez in the Lower Engadine. Zernez is a village that spreads itself over a wide, flat valley bottom where the Inn begins to broaden on its eastward course to Austria and the Danube. It is a place of special interest to naturalists for here came the pioneers of Swiss conservation as long ago as 1909 to negotiate, with the commune of Zernez, the right to set up a nature reserve in a valley to the south of the Inn, the Val Cluoza. Soon other valleys and mountains were added, some in Zernez and others in the neighbouring communes of S-chanf and Scuol. The scheme then won government support and in 1914 the Swiss National Park came into being, a park that now extends along the uplands south of the Inn to include many lovely valleys and forests with peaks rising above them.

It did not come before it was needed, this attempt to protect the wildlife of Switzerland: the game-birds and mammals had long been over-hunted and the flora raped in the craze for growing alpines in gardens, a fashion that spread round the globe in the last quarter of the nineteenth century. Many of the world's mountains were visited by collectors, the European Alps especially. So book after book, article after article, was written not only extolling the glory of the plants of the Alps but also encouraging people to go and uproot them and bring them home. Inevitably the Swiss mountain people began to cash in on the craze. And soon, as the great Swiss authority, Henry Correvon, reported in his *Rock Gardens and Alpine Plants*: 'Lovers of nature were alarmed to mark the ravages committed by collectors; peasants of Savoy or Valais might be seen bringing baskets full of uncommon species for sale in the Geneva market and it was only too certain that several classical habitats for rarities were becoming exhausted. In 1883 a society for the preservation of alpines was formed.' Even so Reginald Farrer, as late as 1913, unblushingly gave instructions in his now classic two-volume work *The English Rock Garden* on how to collect alpines and package and mail them home. Today, with conservation a word on everybody's tongue, we are still far from blameless. I have recently read in a horticultural journal an account of a trip abroad made by a group of gardeners. It ends by describing how they came back 'each with our plastic bags containing the spoils of a truly enjoyable tour'.

There is worldwide confusion about the definition of 'national park'. In some countries it means above all a playground for people but where there is also at least some provision for nature conservation. In other countries a national park is essentially a playground for nature and where human activities are very strictly controlled: what in Britain we would unhesitatingly call a nature reserve. But though we British are clear what we mean by nature reserves we are vague in our interpretation of national parks. Inevitably so. For on other people's definitions—the American for instance—our national parks are neither national nor are they parks: they are for the most part privately owned and they are used for farming, forestry and other purposes.

About the Swiss National Park there is absolutely no uncertainty. It is a strictly run nature reserve where no animal may be hunted, no bird shot, no plant picked, no rock removed, no tree felled. You are allowed in but you must not stray off the trails, camp nor light a fire. In the lyrical words of the official order that gazetted the Park: 'An island of untouched, primitive, natural life is to develop here amid the seething waves of civilization.'

But even in this Arcadia man has not kept his hands entirely behind his back. The brown bear has not been allowed to get a footing in the Park because of the farmers' fear of it spreading to other parts of Switzerland and becoming a menace to domestic animals. Bears occasionally used to stray in from the Italian forests. The last one was shot in 1904 (the last lynx in 1872). This being so I feel that the National Park guide is just a little smug when it claims that 'the wildlife in the Park is not degenerate or effete; the animals do not run begging after the visitors like the bears in America's Yellowstone Park'. At least Yellowstone has kept its bears. All that Switzerland has is the many bear-traps in its museums—witness to how common the brown bear was until fairly recent times. Since the bear is protected in some parts of Europe, even in Italy, a country not famous for nature conservation, has not the time come when the Swiss might consider changing their over-cautious minds?

This National Park in the Canton of the Grisons is essentially a walker's park (there are fifty miles of tracks) but if you are short of time you can get a quick taste of the place by driving along its only motor road. This runs south-east from Zernez up the Spöl valley to the pass called Fiorn (or Ofenpass), one of the minor links between Switzerland and Italy. It is best to stop at Zernez first to see the exhibits and collect the maps and guide-books available at the National Park House. And, in case you can come back at some future date, you may like to note the guided tours you can join to see the Park's fauna and flora under expert tuition. For those who take their mammal-watching seriously there are tours that set out soon after dawn, the best time of day for seeing roe deer and other animals before they retire for the day into the shadows of the forest.

Sooner or later I suppose most visitors to the Park ask the question: why here? Why was this remotest corner of the country made into a Park instead of somewhere more central and convenient, and including higher mountains? The answer is that this area was chosen simply because it was the remotest corner, the least inhabited, the least fertile, the one bit of Switzerland nobody had any use for except conservationists. As Professor Emile Chaix summed it up: 'It could not have been otherwise. How many millions would have been required to compensate the inhabitants of a fertile region if one had wished to take it from them and give it back to Nature to play with?'

So if the naturalists could have had a free choice they might have made their reserve elsewhere. No matter. The Swiss National Park may not be in the finest stretch of the Alps but it is blessed with a fair range of altitudes and aspects and a satisfying variety of soils from crystalline schists for the lime-hating plants to limestone for the calcicoles. And it is sufficiently eastern to include one or two Carpathian species that give its flora a touch of distinction. Among its high-level delights you will find two pure-white buttercups, *Ranunculus alpestris* and *R. parnassifolius*; the yellow whitlow-grass, *Draba aizoides*, which I once saw under distinctly alpine conditions (a March snowstorm) on the limestone cliffs of south Wales; its white-flowered relative, *D. tomentosa*; purple saxifrage (*Saxifraga oppositifolia*) to remind you of British mountains; *Androsace helvetica* whose compact cushions erupt all over with white stars; the granite-loving *A. glacialis* whose flowers may be white, pink or carmine; and *Soldanella pusilla*, lilac gem of the eastern Swiss snow-line. But seek further and you will come upon many other treasures, some of great rarity, to be enjoyed here in their wildness, to be admired, described, drawn or photographed and then left undisturbed in what is their only right place in the world.

It is along the Ofenpass road that follows the winding Spöl up from Zernez that you come in a few miles to one of the entrances to the Park. A notice in Romansh, the local language for whose survival its speakers have long and successfully campaigned, reads: 'Parc Naziunal Svizzer: Protectziun absoluta da flora e fauna,' from which you will see that Romansh is a sort of Italian with a fondness for zeds. If it is the middle of a summer's day you are not likely to see much of the fauna; but the flora will be there, especially higher up where the forest begins to thin. On roadside rocks you will find the red flowers of the alpenrose (*Rhododendron hirsutum*) which tells you that you are on limestone: it is a crumbling dolomitic limestone that has weathered into the sharp, deeply gullied peaks you see all round.

Near the top of the pass the road is edged with level swards coloured with flowers of small stature: round-leaved wintergreen, frog orchid, felwort, alpine aster and grass of Parnassus—these are everywhere. Tiny gentians of intense blue are scattered all through the turf among orange hawkweeds, pale pink and white mountain everlasting (*Antennaria dioica*), deep pink cushions of soap wort (*Saponaria ocymoides*), and the rosy pink calcicole heather, *Erica herbacea* (*carnea*), well known in British gardens. Beyond these flowery levels, junipers and young pines lead into taller forests farther back. Whether above the forests you will see snowy mountain shoulders gleaming in the sun will depend on the season. In a late year snow lies on these peaks till early August. But sooner or later it practically all disappears from even the highest summits of the Park (though there are small permanent glaciers). From this pass you get a superb view south to the Italian Alps, a great sweep of snowy peaks with countless miles of forest folded along their flanks—one of the finest wilderness areas left in Europe, a worthy place for the brown bear to be allowed to survive in.

Once you have decided to see the Park on foot it scarcely matters which of the routes you choose. They all lead you up through superb country, usually at first through conifer forest then on to open slopes and ridges. The western side of the Park is dominated by Piz Quattervals (10,366 feet), and its sister heights—an imposingly jagged group rising 4,000 feet clear above the forest. We approached it from S-chanf up the Muschauns valley. The air was fresh after a morning's rain as the forest track took us gently higher and higher above the river. From a near-by meadow marmots whistled like Welsh shepherds and for a while we watched them feeding and playing among the rocks—dark, round-headed, furry, rather otter-like. One was digging vigorously, throwing out earth with its hind legs. As we got near there were more whistles of alarm and most of the marmots scampered down slopes into holes. The young were less cautious: one we could have picked up before it responded at last to the frenzied whistles of its mother and vanished down a burrow at our feet.

After the dismal conifer plantations of Britain with their poverty of ground flora, what a dreamlike experience it was to walk among these well-spaced alpine spruces and find a wealth of wildflowers all through the forest, especially in the glades. There were treasures like the single-flowered wintergreen (*Moneses uniflora*) with its solitary, large, pure white, down-looking bloom; stately blue spikes of Jacob's ladder; clumps of the yellow crucifer (*Biscutella laevigata*), that has the English name of buckler mustard from the flat shape of the seed-pods; the orange and purple flowers of alpine toadflax (*Linaria alpina*); yellow globe-flowers colouring wet gullies; showy deep purple pea-flowers of the alpine sainfoin (*Hedysarum hedysaroides*). And we had the good luck to find one plant of alpine clematis still showing its last lilac flowers though we had feared it would be quite over. A further delight was the twin flower (*Linnaea borealis*) whose hanging pink bells we saw clustered in shady, wet places: a plant especially dear to lovers of alpines both for its own sake and for Linnaeus whose memory it helps to keep green.

We came clear of the forest. The fang of Piz Quattervals rose splendidly ahead; and across the valley we examined the bare slopes of Piz d'Esan for signs of life. At first we saw nothing. But how often it's like that when you look for animals or plants.

A subtle focusing of mind and eye is needed before you begin to find anything. We realized at last that there were in fact groups, some of them quite large groups, of red deer, chamois and ibex scattered up the rough mountainside. We set up the telescope and found the red deer first. They might have been posed by an artist or a photographer, lying in attractive rows up the steep slope, peacefully chewing the cud after their dawn feeding. Most were stags with fine antlers from which the velvet hung in rags. In contrast the little chamois were quite lively, feeding as they moved across the hillside; and suddenly one of the females went racing down the slope, we couldn't see why, followed closely by a young one. As for the ibex (which are also called bouquetin, steinbock and capricorn) they stood where ibex ought to stand—on a skyline of rock with their great curved horns outlined against white clouds. These magnificent grey goats of the mountains, of which there are now hundreds in the Park, were introduced here from Italy in 1920. Presumably long ago they were common all over the Swiss uplands, judging by their frequent appearance in Swiss heraldry and on inn signs. (Though perhaps this argument is not all that strong when you think of all the lions on the inn signs in Britain!)

It was while scanning the crags for ibex that we discovered two golden eagles perched on a pinnacle far above us. Young ones evidently, just able to fly, for when a third eagle came soaring over the valley at their level they flew rather unsteadily to meet it, then followed it closely back to the crag as if in the hope of being fed. But despite all the great cliffs in this highly protected, animal-rich Park, eagles are not common here, nor ravens either. There was a time, I suppose, when there were also lammergeiers in the Engadine. If so they have been shot out long since. And how can we expect shepherds not to look askance at a bird so named? For to anyone with a knowledge of German the lammergeier is the 'lamb-vulture'—an unfortunate name for so innocuous a bird. Perhaps we should drop this damning name forthwith and stick to 'bearded vulture'.

Much of this Park is under natural forest—larches, spruces, pines and junipers fill the valleys and clamber over the ridges between. And of all these conifers the one most people want to see is cembra pine, also called Swiss stone pine but more often the Arolla pine (from the name of the long-popular resort under the Dent Blanche and the Matterhorn in the Pennine Alps). Though the cembra pine grows in many parts of mountain Switzerland I can scarcely think it can be anywhere finer than in the National Park where there are especially superb stands of it along the eastern boundary from S-charl up the valley to the Tamangur Forest. Here the trees, little exploited, have reached a great age and size, some tall and straight but many twisted, gnarled and weather-beaten. This is a pine of world ecological importance for its forests extend not only across the Alps but eastwards across hundreds of miles of Siberia (hence its other name of Siberian cedar). It is far from being renowned for its timber but the Swiss have used it in their houses: it is said to be unshrinking and pleasantly scented.

Despite the cembra pine's vast range there are people who believe it is past its heyday, an ancient species on its way out of the world. Certainly Reginald Farrer thought so. In his flowery way he wrote in *Alpines and Bog Plants* (describing a walk up the valley towards Arolla): 'The great excitement at this part of the ascent is one's first sight of the Arolla pine. About all waning, dying species there hangs a flavour of almost Stuart romance; but *Pinus cembra* is the protagonist of nature's tragedy in the Alps . . . a very ancient species being crowded out of the woods by younger species.' Whether that is Farrer romance rather than Stuart romance I must leave you to decide. What is certain is that the large wingless seeds of the Arolla pine are of great importance as a food supply. They are as sweet and nutritious as hazel nuts and in Siberia are collected in quantities by the peasants. In the Alps they are left for the many animals and birds that eagerly seek them. Among the animals are red squirrels and smaller rodents, foxes and deer. In Siberia bears also eat them and the Siberian squirrel is very dependent on them. The bird most addicted is the nutcracker which has a bill with a cavity in the upper mandible and a projection in the lower—a natural nutcracking tool useful in breaking the hard shells in which these seeds are encased.

Nutcrackers are one of the chief delights of the Park. You can be quite alone in the July silence of the cembra pines, a silence that seems emphasized by the occasional chirruping of crested tits in the tree tops, when suddenly your grove is invaded by a noisy troop of nutcrackers in search of mature cones. These have to be attacked with real vigour because they do not open and release their seeds naturally as those of many conifers do. The nut-cracker's far-carrying call is a harsh, somewhat jay-like 'kraak-kraak'. Their flight, too, is floppy and jay-like. So is their way of coming to earth to bury food, by which habit they presumably played as great a part in the original spread of the cembra pine forest as jays played elsewhere in the post-glacial spreading of the oak. In one respect the nutcracker differs from the jay: he is much more likely to perch conspicuously and long enough for you to get details of his neatly white-spotted brown plumage and white-ended black tail. These nutcrackers of the Alps and the Car-pathians are the thick-billed race, like those of Scandinavia. The only difference is in diet—in Scandinavia they have to manage without the seeds of *Pinus cembra* and there they eat the seeds of other conifers and lots more hazel nuts and other fruits. The nut-cracker that occasionally invades western Europe including Britain is the thin-billed race that comes from Siberia when the cembra pine seed crop fails there, as happens at irregular intervals. All we need in Britain is a few forests of cembra pines and I'm sure it would not be long before we had our own population of nutcrackers. (Forestry Commission, please note.)

Among other birds of the Swiss National Park that British bird-watchers usually want to see are citril finch (best seen when feeding on the ground in forest glades), crag martin (breeding in rocks along the Ofenpass road and elsewhere), black woodpecker (a few only and hard to find), three-toed woodpecker (which pecks out cavities and rings on tree trunks to get at the sap), honey buzzard (as elusive here as everywhere else) and Bonelli's warbler (whose feeble, music-less song can be heard round the lower edges of the forest in spring and early summer). One bird you probably will not tick off on your list is the eagle-owl. It hides in thick trees by day and seldom calls except in winter and very early spring. In fact it gets its breeding season over while the mountain forests are cut off by deep snow and little is therefore known about its nesting behaviour. But that is good and proper. Such mysteries enrich us, somehow adding a dimension to our lives.

We left the National Park immensely thankful that the Swiss conservationists had been early enough in the field to save these forests and mountains before the age of popular tourism. Otherwise by now they might well be thoroughly commercialized. Both Davos and St. Moritz, remember, are only about twenty miles away. And the most devoted admirer of the Swiss must surely admit that in their anxiety to make their country the world's playground they must soon be in danger of overdoing the hotels, restaurants, cafés, holiday chalets, funiculars, ski-lifts, entertainments, souvenir shanties and sellers of sprigs of edelweiss. So it is all the more merciful to find that in this one corner of their land they have abstained totally from exercising their talent for promoting tourism. Here, for sixty-five square miles, there is peace from it all. Peace even from cow-bells or, as some may say, peace especially from cow-bells.

We said a reluctant good-bye to Zernez and its mountains and forests. Along the banks of the Inn black redstarts and white wagtails flitted among the rocks; and about a hundred Alpine choughs chirruped (their sound deserves no better description) from the roof of the timber-yard. We drove through St. Moritz and in another few miles turned right for the Julier pass and, for a change, a landscape of granite. On our left rose a summit that has the distinction of giving rise to three streams, one of which flows east to the Danube, one north to the Rhine and one south to the Po. In half a gale we picnicked at the top of the Julier pass, crouching in the shelter of rock to keep the wind off our tiny meths stove. No time to botanize but from where we sat we could see vanilla orchid, moss campion, round-headed rampion, many hawkweeds and large-sized daisies as well as juniper and heather.

From the pass we dropped into the deep valley of the Julia river, with high walls that looked granitic climbing away on

each side. No finer valley than this had we seen in all Switzerland. At Tiefencastel, where the Julia flows into the Albula, we
turned left along the road to Thusis and were soon obviously
back on to limestone, for quite suddenly the roadsides were blue
with chicory and salvia. For miles we followed limestone gorges
into whose flanks the road has here and there been cut and
colonnaded by bold engineering. Then over the Hinterrhein at
Thusis and on to Reichenau, so completing a circle, for we had
passed through there on our way to the east.

Though daylight was fading when we reached Andermatt we
drove on because we wanted to get nearer to Interlaken that night.
So up the zigzags of the Furka pass, in and out of treacherous
patches of mist. We crawled miserably over the top in dense cloud
and felt our way down the other side, rather terrified and wishing
we had pitched our tent at Andermatt. Then the dreamlike experience of emerging abruptly from the mist and finding the great
crevassed ice terraces of the Rhône glacier hanging above us
bright in the moonlight. Quickly the mist closed in again: but in
those few minutes we had seen something altogether beautiful
that would go with us for the rest of our lives.

We struggled on through the fog all the winding way to the
bottom of the valley and up the endless hairpins of the other side
and over the Grimsel pass with visibility down to a yard or so for
miles. But down and down we zigzagged and so came clear of the
mist at last. Still far short of Interlaken, and not knowing where
we were, we found a quiet lane and camped on the first open
patch of level verge.

We woke early next morning to see the sun just touching the
snow with pink on the peak of the Ritzlihorn. We found, as usual,
that we had camped in a flowery spot. The laneside all round us
was splendid with yellow salvia, dark mullein (is there a finer
mullein than this?), white rock-lily (*Anthericum ramosum*) and the
big yellow flowers of the touch-me-not balsam (*Impatiens noli-
tangere*). A female red-backed shrike perched on the nearest bush,
now and then dropping to the ground to take a grasshopper
which she transferred from beak to claw in order to dismember
it.

We came down the valley to Innertkirchen and were soon at Interlaken. On the Briezersee great crested grebes sailed and dived, remarkably indifferent to the crowd of people and boats. Black-headed gulls weaved about over the lake, snapping at flying ants. And behind the gulls stretched the skyline of snowy peaks that culminate in the triple summit of Eiger, Monch and Jungfrau. But too soon our holiday was nearing its end and we had not yet seen the Jura . . .

We took the Geneva road. At Chateau d'Oex we regretted that the month was July, for this little town lies under the botanically rich Pays d'Enhaut which is famous for its narcissi that whiten the hillsides in spring, an event about which a leaflet from the Swiss Tourist Office let itself go with some abandon: 'The scene best known to the public in the Vaudois Alps, is that of the fields of *Narcissus poeticus*, fields visited in May and June by such crowds as oblige the steamboat and railway companies to organize a special service. The mountainsides, from Montreux to Chateau d'Oex, are besieged by admirers of these immense, scented stretches of whiteness. Above all, it is the Pays d'Enhaut that is privileged in this regard. In May and June the hillside pastures are so covered with the immaculate drapery as to suggest fallen snow. From Vevey to the Col de Jaman all is equally white; but here as summer approaches, the perfumed invasion gradually ascends until it reaches the cols where the alpine flora proper is just disclosing itself. The anemones and gentians then step into possession . . .'

Between Lausanne and Geneva the long wooded flanks of the Jura built up rapidly in the north. We turned off the main road at Nyon and climbed up through lanes to camp in a pasture where the farmlands ended and mixed forests began to clamber up the slopes. We looked back across a pattern of grassy fields and hedges that might have been somewhere along the Welsh border. Each hour the chimes of six village clocks came up to us from the valley, ten minutes elapsing between the first and the last. In the turf round our tent grew an abundance of spiked speedwell, Nottingham catchfly and a delightful pink quite rightly called *Dianthus superbus* (for the sake of which we have ever since grown in our garden a deliciously scented pink called Rainbow Loveliness, which is a cultivated variety of *D. superbus*).

Dusk falls early on this eastern side of the Jura. We watched the shadows spread from our forest-edge camp down across the farmlands to the near edge of Lake Geneva, then on across the water to the feet of the French Alps. Mont Blanc, which all day had been a scarcely visible grey hump, now rose brilliantly clear above its neighbours as its great snowfields turned pink in the level rays of the sun. It seemed almost to be floating, high and unreal, above the rest of the Alps. And though it gradually faded it remained visible, still faintly glowing pink, two hours after deep darkness had fallen among the pines around our tent.

Hilarious laughter woke us at five next morning. It came from a green woodpecker on a tree a few yards from our tent. Was it an ominous sound, we wondered. For as every countryman knows, hilarity from this woodpecker presages rain. And when we looked out we could see great sagging clouds streaming down off the Jura from the west. Soon the rain began, heavy and getting worse all the time. Field-work being unthinkable we took ourselves off to Geneva and spent the afternoon on a dripping tour of the famous Botanic Garden, 'the Mecca of botanical science' our guide-book called it. There, along with plants from all over the world, we found the flora of several European mountain ranges grouped in geographical and ecological order, so that the Jura plants, those of the central Alps, those of the eastern Alps and so on, were each in their separate groups, with sub-divisions for limestone and granite species: and all growing among terraced rocks that gave a fair imitation of nature. As most of the plants were labelled we spent several useful though very wet hours identifying some that had puzzled us on our way through Switzerland. Finally the garden's staff, no doubt unable to believe that anyone could be out in that appalling rain, went home without bothering to clear the grounds. So we found ourselves locked in and could only escape by climbing out over the fence. It wasn't a great problem but it might have taken a little explaining if we had jumped into the arms of a policeman.

After the trough the ridge. Next morning was perfect from the moment we woke. We breakfasted in warm sunshine with crested tits churring all round and crossbills constantly passing overhead. Then we followed a rough track that went winding up through a splendid beech forest that climbs high up this side of the Jura and yields to spruces only a few hundred feet from the top of the ridge. Above the conifers we came out to the open mountain where we walked and botanized happily for the rest of the day. The limestone flora was colourful and varied: there were orchids everywhere, and gentians, rockroses, saxifrages, daphnes, anemones, campanulas, pansies and endless other treasures, all enjoying life up there in the mountain air.

Often from the spruce forest just below we could hear the sharp calls of citril finches and occasionally small parties of them came flying up the slopes to feed on the seeds of lady's mantle and other mountain plants. But they were difficult birds to approach, being quick to warn each other with their 'twayee' alarm note that reminded us of the redpolls of the conifer woods back home. New animals for us were the handsome yellow and black wall-lizards that scuttled about over the rocks, probably catching the bright emerald grasshoppers that were extremely common and noisy on that warm sheltered flank of the ridge.

Slowly making our way from one flowery ledge to another we came up to the breezy crest of the Jura and looked westwards into France across a vast forest landscape, ridge after tree-covered ridge billowing into the distance. But not an unrelieved blanket of forest: the trees in the foreground looked well spaced; and everywhere there were natural breaks where rocky outcrops stood above the trees or where gorges with high limestone precipices had split the face of the land. This westward view from the Jura would certainly be one of the acknowledged great prospects of Europe were it not that from this same ridge the view east to the line of the Alps is among the most celebrated of all. But for me the forests of the west slopes of Jura were more alluring than those icy peaks far in the east.

We came down off the summit, glad to get out of the wind into the warm world of lizards, grasshoppers and butterflies. We looked for the last time at all those limestone flowers and wondered what man-made threats might lie ahead for them. One little thing comforted us—the leaflet of the Swiss Tourist Office rhapsodizing about the mountain flora. Its English is a little bizarre: 'It is to the Jura you must go fully to enjoy fields of anemones and gentians and *Daphne cneorum* which will act as magic upon your emotions,' but at least it showed that the Swiss are fully aware of the precious quality of their mountain flora. If their emotions truly are aroused by the sight of their wildflowers then there is far better hope for conservation of the Swiss flora than there is for that of many other countries.

4. Chronicles from the Parish Pump

Ever since 16 November 1906, the *Guardian* has published a daily paragraph called 'A Country Diary'. It is a rural peephole for a journal whose main windows overlook the affairs of urban man, the world of business and finance, and the international scene. Right from my teens I was a regular reader of the *Guardian* (then the *Manchester Guardian*). By which I mean that I used to see it in the local library, read 'A Country Diary' and ignore the rest. My favourite diarist then was A.W.B. who wrote from Cheshire and seemed to devote his life to spotting rare birds on the local meres or in north Wales where his particular spot was Malltraeth Pool in Anglesey. I never met A.W.B. but after years of reading his diaries I did venture to write to him about an osprey I saw over the Dyfi estuary. I addressed my letter to A.W.B., c/o The Manchester Guardian and in due course he replied. So instead of three initials he became a name: A. W. Boyd, who is best remembered now as the author of *A Country Parish*, an excellent study of the natural history of his home parish of Great Budworth in Cheshire. I am happy to think that nearby Rostherne Mere, one of his favourite waters, has become a National Nature Reserve where people go to watch birds from the A. W. Boyd Memorial Observatory.

When I was invited to join the Country Diary team in 1957 the features editor gave me one instruction only—to make the topics as wide-ranging as possible except that I was not to write about birds. This last was a tough condition to impose on a compulsive bird-watcher but I could see his point of view: birds just then truly were an overdone theme in books and magazines. There was also a sparkling radio programme devoted entirely to them—James Fisher's monthly 'Birds in Britain'. There is a better balance now that we are learning to look at nature more as a whole. I obeyed the 'no birds' ruling for a long time until readers began to write me sarcastic letters asking if there are no birds in Wales? Since then I have often written about birds in the diary and, for all I know, it would be news to the present features editor that a 'no birds' condition ever existed.

My first diary appeared under the dateline 'Machynlleth, 9 October'. And 'Machynlleth', though the town is eight miles away in the next county, has been the first word of my diary ever since, simply because, for the convenience of the post office, it is part of my address. In that first diary I wrote of autumn in the garden: Michaelmas daisies, a specially scented sedum and tobacco flowers —these were all attracting many butterflies and moths in a spell of halcyon weather. Next week the idyll continued. I wrote sitting outside with the sun hot on my bare arms while a woodlark carolled overhead. Happy days. Only six years later the beautifully voiced woodlark, till then so common and taken for granted, had gone entirely from the district, a victim of the cruel winter of 1962–3. The following week I was still in the garden, writing now in praise of fieldmice, and it was not until 30 October that I got a few yards beyond the garden gate, found an old birch full of goat-moth holes and spoke about the curious way their scent attracts red admiral butterflies. In November I pronounced that the occupation of our district by the grey squirrel was now complete. (This process had taken two years since the first one was seen here.) I wrote of goats on the hills of north Wales; rhapsodized about walking up Rhinog; discussed rowan-tree superstitions and quoted John Evelyn on rowan-beer ('an incomparable drink' he called it); and I ended the year with an account of a blue or mountain hare seen in Merioneth (but was it a good record?).

The next year, amongst other things, I castigated naturalists' widows who throw away their husbands' nature diaries instead of offering them to the local library or nature trust. This outburst was occasioned when I rescued the last two of a local naturalist's diaries from an outhouse where the rest—the product of a life-time's jottings—had already rotted away. As a diarist myself I read the two surviving volumes with the utmost interest and mourned deeply the loss of all the rest. So can I appeal here and now to anyone who possesses old nature or any other diaries to offer them to some organization for safe keeping? You yourself may not find them exciting but it could well be that other people, perhaps long years ahead, will be totally fascinated by them. The notes Uncle George made when bug-hunting on Aran Fawddwy in 1895 may be quoted with wonder, love and praise in the entomological literature of 2095.

Though grey squirrels now possessed our parish the reds were still around. At least until spring 1958 I saw them almost daily from the garden of our hillside cottage and was still finding plenty of their nests. On 2 April, my diary relates, I watched one running along the bank of the Einion river for a long way, carrying a bunch of moss in her mouth. She then crossed over on a foot-bridge and went all the way back along the ground on the other side of the stream. I have never decided why she went so far round when all she needed to do to cross the water was to go by way of the over-arching boughs of the nearest tree. A few weeks later I met with an otter that also behaved very strangely. I was bird-watching in the middle of the Dyfi estuary. The tide was out and through binoculars, half a mile away, I could see this otter eating something on a sand-bank at the edge of a creek. To observe an otter in the broad light of day was unusual enough. But to my further surprise he allowed me to walk to within thirty yards before he slid off into the water and vanished, leaving his meal behind, which I could now see was a large flatfish. As I walked forward to examine this fish, the otter, to my astonishment, re-emerged from the water, came up the bank, quite casually picked up the fish, stopped to eye me with what seemed like curiosity, then swam away. It was an incident I shall treasure always for events like that only happen once in a lifetime.

The year 1959 was the year of the drought. It was also the year when Penny and I came to live at Ynys Edwin and so had the pleasure of getting used to a world of peat bogs edged by tangled woods and broken up by tree-covered outcrops of slaty rock. It was a very quiet little region, a home for snipe and curlew, a wilderness of rushes and gorse. We could have believed it hadn't

I *Top* (*a*), the house by the marsh. Called Ynys Edwin (Edwin's Island), the site was no doubt once surrounded by the swamps and morasses of the great bog of Cors Fochno. *Bottom* (*b*), Cors Fochno today. Formerly of much greater extent, Cors Fochno (Borth Bog) is still a sizeable boggy wilderness and is a National Nature Reserve

2 *Top* (*a*), Dyfi Furnace, between Machynlleth and Aberystwyth. A silver-lead refinery in the seventeenth century, it became an iron smeltery in the eighteenth. A listed ancient monument, it is seen here before restoration. *Bottom* (*b*), oak woodland of the sort which was widely cleared to provide charcoal to fire the furnace. The woodland fragments that survive are mostly like this one, given over to sheep grazing with no regeneration either of trees or undergrowth

3 Snowdonia National Park. *Top (a)*, Snowdon from the east. *Bottom left (b)*, purple saxifrage, a common plant on Snowdon, sometimes flowering as early as February (note the icicles). *Bottom right (c)*, mountain avens, another arctic-alpine but very rare in Snowdonia

4 The Swiss National Park. In the east of the country, this park is a strictly controlled nature reserve. *Top left* (*a*), the peak called Piz Madlain. *Top right* (*b*), an Arolla pine (*Pinus cembra*) of which fine old specimens exist in the park. *Bottom* (*c*), the nutcracker lives very largely on Arolla pine seeds

5   Changing Welsh uplands. *Top* (*a*), since World War I large areas of the
Welsh hills have been planted with alien conifers as here at Soar-y-mynydd, south-
east of Tregaron. *Bottom* (*b*), ever since the last century more and more large
reservoirs have invaded the hills and further ones are planned. Photograph
shows Nant-y-moch reservoir with Plynlimon beyond

6 Mecca for botanists in Clare. The Burren, a region of almost bare limestone in western Ireland, is famous for its colourful wildflowers some of which are rarities. *Top* (*a*), a typical Burren hill. *Bottom left* (*b*), dense-flowered orchid which in Britain is found only in this part of Ireland. *Bottom right* (*c*), spring gentian which makes patches of intense blue in May

7   Birds of prey in Spain. *Top* (*a*), the Spanish imperial eagle is now very rare. *Bottom* (*b*), griffon, Egyptian and black vultures on the Coto Doñana. Eagles, vultures and many other birds of prey in Europe are in urgent need of conservation

8   More Coto Doñana birds. This magnificent reserve is famous for its nesting colonies of spoonbills, *top* (*a*), and little egrets, *bottom* (*b*)

changed in many centuries. But then, my diary of 8 April reminds me, a chance remark by an old man of the village completely changed our view of the scene. A century or more ago, he said, all round these marshes were scattered cottages of the sort that, being built in one night, could claim squatters' rights. We looked round us with fresh eyes. Gone now was the wilderness. Instead we had to visualize a populous community somehow getting a living off this unpromising land, some of them perhaps inhabiting mud-walled cottages that have long since dissolved without trace except for the hollies planted near them to break the worst of the estuary winds.

This year, 1959, was also the year of the thorn apple. The long hot sunny days caused this poisonous but handsome weed with pale-purple, trumpet-shaped flowers, to spring up in unexpected places in many parts of Britain, including our new garden at Ynys Edwin. Its sudden appearance in so many different localities was apparently because its seeds were a frequent though unintentional constituent of poultry corn imported from abroad. Probably some had lain in the ground many years waiting for a Mediterranean type of summer to germinate them. Certainly our predecessors at Ynys Edwin had kept chickens and so unknowingly bequeathed to us a most interesting plant. Curiously, though subsequent summers fell far short of 1959's splendid record, the thorn apple continued to seed itself in our garden for about the next ten years. Another curious plant came my way that year—the umbellifer called spignel. I had begun to collect material for *The Snowdonia National Park* and was shown the white flowers of this attractive herb in a meadow of Tir Stent on the north side of Cadair Idris. Though I enjoyed seeing spignel it did not seem at the time to be a plant of outstanding significance. Yet of all the wildflowers I touched on in that book or in my diaries in the *Guardian* the spignel has brought me most letters: mainly from people interested in seeing the plant in the field. It is one of the pleasantest by-products of writing about nature—this discovering of the odd things that unexpectedly interest people.

Over the years I have seen two hoopoes in Wales, one in the north, the other in the south, if you agree with the tradition that

E

the Dyfi estuary is the dividing line between the two regions. It was on 1 June 1960, that I wrote about my first hoopoe. Friends living on a farm above Harlech had lately been hearing a hoopoe's notes in the dawn-chorus. So an early-morning party of us went there one weekend and sat on the hillside near the farmhouse. Waiting on a Welsh hillside listening to curlews and lapwings, buzzards and ravens, it seemed totally unreal that we were hoping to hear a hoopoe. But that only made the bird's eventual appearance the more delightful. There suddenly he was, on the nearest tree-top, shouting his outlandish 'poo-poop' before he flew off towards the inland hills.

As the Country Diaries are of a conveniently quotable length it occasionally happens that editors of books and magazines write for permission to use them. My diary for 18 May 1960, was a moral tale and so found a place in an instruction book for the young. A local forestry worker sent me word that he had found a cuckoo's egg in a hedge-sparrow's nest. When I went to see it I found him and his mates debating a most interesting ethical problem over their lunch. One side said that the cuckoo's egg ought to be destroyed. Their argument was that by so doing you would take only one life and that instantaneously. Whereas if you leave the cuckoo's egg to hatch you are condemning a brood of young hedge-sparrows to a slow death. The other side dismissed this attitude as sentimental, pointing out that it wasn't man's fault if nature used such crude means of reproducing cuckoos. Anyway, they said, it would be extremely interesting to see a young cuckoo grow up. Fifteen men discussed this grave matter and concluded by putting the matter to the vote. Six were for non-interference but nine reckoned the cuckoo's egg should be destroyed. And so it was. But was this really a wise decision? I wonder what the majority opinion was among the children who considered this question in school?

One of my diaries for January 1961 put in a plea for the otter and other mammals. I had been very annoyed to find in our local paper an advertisement by a firm of furriers asking for the skins of otters, badgers, polecats, hares, rabbits and stoats. But judging by the high price offered, an otter skin was clearly the great prize.

I asked the old question that never seems to get answered: why are we so unbalanced in our attitude to wildlife, lavishing endless protection on most birds yet hardly raising a finger to conserve the mammals? Today things are beginning to move very slightly. There is some degree of protection for the badger. But the otter, though greatly decreased, is still unprotected by any law. Why? Who is it we are afraid to offend if we were to protect the otter?

Another face of the exploitation of wildlife was the revival of falconry. I received a letter from a Shropshire falconer asking me if I could help him to get a young peregrine. I pointed out to him that peregrines were protected birds, that they were apparently declining and that in any case I felt that a peregrine, the quintessence of wildness and freedom, should stay wild and free and not be tethered to a block of wood for somebody's amusement. In 1961 we began to count the number of peregrines breeding in Britain. It was a census whose results were to shock the birdwatchers of this country as never before. For it showed that quite suddenly the peregrine had suffered a truly catastrophic decline in numbers. Though we didn't realize it at the time this peregrine census was a turning point in the history of natural history. Till then only a minority of naturalists were deeply involved in conservation. But the sudden decline of the peregrine, quickly followed by severe losses in other creatures, caused by the widespread use of agricultural pesticides, taught us all how suddenly and totally the world of nature can be threatened in the technological age. From then on many naturalists began to devote most of their time and energies to conservation and have gone on doing so.

In January 1962, I walked up to one of the higher farms of our parish, happened to meet the shepherd and stood chatting with him outside his house. He was a great one for seeking the signs of spring, this man. Into his ragged old cap every April he pinned the first bunch he found of what he called *penllwyd* ('grey head'), in other words the cotton sedge—its buds are grey before they open into yellow flowers which in their turn are followed by fluffy white seed heads. But now it was January and he pointed to the sprouting leaves of snowdrops in his tiny garden. Not that he saw in them a signal of spring nor even in the flowers that would be showing next month. For him spring would be on its way only when he saw honey bees at his snowdrops. As I remarked in my diary, I suspect that the sight of those bees really brought him a delight that was deeper than the simple anticipation of spring. For there is in many a peasant heart an ancestral respect for bees, honey having been since earliest times regarded as a food of sacred origin. This meant that beekeepers and mead-makers were held in the highest respect. At the Welsh court under the laws of the tenth-century king, Hywel Dda, mead-makers enjoyed considerable privileges.

This shepherd I spoke to was skilled in herbal remedies, not only for himself but for his stock also. And though I daresay some of his potions were not as effective as he believed, I am sure he did less harm than those modern shepherds who are never without their hypodermic syringes and inject their animals with all sorts of drugs without the least real knowledge of what they are about. My shepherd friend not only thought that animal husbandry was entering a dangerous phase with an over-use of drugs, he was also opposed to the ploughing up of old herb-rich pastures and replacing them by modern seed-mixtures. He saw the disappearance of herb-rich fields and the prevalence of disease in modern animals as two ends of a chain that lacked no links whatsoever.

I am afraid some of my diaries have left the reader rather depressed. But is it my fault if I can remember oak woodlands that stretched for colourful miles along Welsh valleysides that are now prickly with dense black thickets of Sitka spruce? Or if I can remember the Clywedog winding through a peaceful, wild and totally beautiful valley that in 1962 was about to be drowned behind a very high dam? I say now what I said then—that we could more easily endure these losses if some known limit had been set to them. But we are left in the dark as to how many more square miles of conifers are to be allocated to Wales, how many more valleys will be drowned. This very day I read in the paper that the Elan valley is threatened with having to accommodate the biggest reservoir in Europe. Heaven spare me from having to live downstream from a dam of that size. It would need more than a geologist's assurance to convince me that there can never be an earthquake in the Silurian rocks of central Wales. Boffins are sometimes wrong.

Guardian readers quite often write to the country diarists, agreeing with them, or disagreeing and trying to educate them. September 1963 brought me a most interesting letter from a man who was allergic to spiders. I had expressed the opinion that people's revulsion at the sight of spiders was unlikely to be a genuine allergy and was usually acquired by imitation at an early age of the ridiculous attitudes of their parents towards the 'creepy-crawly' world. I therefore suggested that teachers of nature study could do a great service by facing up to this problem of 'nasty' creatures by showing to children the beauty and wonder of the lives of insects and spiders. But now this reader from Liverpool convinced me I may have been wrong. He explained that, regretfully aware of his own spider-fear, he made every effort to prevent his daughter from acquiring it. So though spiders made him shudder he bravely used to invite his infant daughter to inspect spiders and their webs with him and, to use his own words: 'Never did I let her see that I disliked the creatures.' Despite these precautions, at about three years old the child suddenly showed fear of spiders, a fear she had retained ever since though she was now grown up and had become a biologist. Therefore, my correspondent concluded, there must be something innate about these phobias and that I had been wrong to suppose that they are mainly acquired by children imitating their parents. He also doubted if the correct teaching of nature study could do much to dispel these fears. Knowledge and appreciation of the beauty of spiders' webs had done nothing to eliminate the horror of spiders either for him or his daughter.

Remember National Nature Week, 18–25 May 1963? When it was announced, with its decorative nature stamps, its attractive nature exhibitions, its many nature walks and nature talks, this Week must have seemed to the general public as a bit of frivolity for heralding in the spring. People probably thought that if so many naturalists were feeling like skipping lambs it would do no harm if they were allowed to show it. But when National Nature Week arrived its message was not at all of spring except in the sense of Rachel Carson's silent one. It was a story of pollution and pesticides spreading through the land and wiping out birds, animals and plants on a massive scale. Certainly all this had been said before: but now the earth had given a lurch and from about 1963 onwards conservationists began to find that people were actually listening when told that the world of nature and the world of man are the same world and that if wild creatures were dying because their environment was no longer habitable then man had better look to the safety of his. As I ended my diary of 6 March: 'Man's whole future depends on his acquiring a saner attitude to nature than he holds at present. If National Nature Week can help however little towards alerting the public on this point it will have been well worth while.'

The winter of 1963–4 Penny and I spent in Northern Rhodesia (which changed its name to Zambia about that time). So I bade farewell to Country Diary readers in September 1963, rather expecting the editor would use this break as an opportunity of ridding the paper of my particular brand of doom, gloom and belly-aching. To my surprise I was admitted back into the fold on my return home in March, and duly celebrated my first diary of the year by contrasting the wealth of birds of prey in Africa with their scarcity in most of western Europe. Agricultural poisons had made a clean sweep of such birds across vast areas of cultivated country and now, I complained, it was the turn of the mountain districts. 'Already', I said, 'the peregrine is on the way out and now the golden eagle in Scotland and the red kite in Wales both look doomed if the poison at present employed in sheep dips is not very soon discontinued.' How some readers of 'A Country Diary' must have groaned and wished I had stayed in Africa!

That spring brought an item of good news: part of Snowdon was to be a National Nature Reserve. But I still think now what I said then—that it ought not to have been necessary to make Snowdon a reserve at all, because being part of a National Park ought to be sufficient protection. This will not happen until we get legislation that will make National Parks far more secure than at present against commercial and industrial exploitation of all kinds. In Snowdonia a good first step after that would be the removal of the railway up Snowdon. Not that I have anything against people having fun on narrow-gauge lines: but that particular railway means that the top of Snowdon is grossly over-visited and is unspeakably degraded as a result. The top of the highest peak in southern Britain deserves a better fate.

I see from my diary of 18 March 1964, that this was the year when the North Wales Naturalists' Trust appealed for money to save the beautiful woodlands of the Vale of Ffestiniog, a place whose reputation for scenic splendour goes back for two centuries. One eighteenth-century traveller let his enthusiasm go so far as to declare that in this valley 'the romantic beauties of nature are so singular and extravagant that they are scarcely to be conceived by those who have confined their curiosity to other parts of Britain'. The Vale of Ffestiniog still keeps its verdure and beauty. The broad slow stream winds through its pastures to the estuary. The waterfalls are as they have always been. And if whole hillsides are even today covered with broad-leaved trees with hardly a conifer in sight it is only because people responded magnificently to the Trust's appeal. The money was raised and these woodlands are now a nature reserve. Not that it ought to have been necessary, all this frenetic begging-bowl act. If National Park status had any real meaning the destruction of those fine woodlands would have been forbidden by law.

The year 1965 was memorable. It was the year of the 'Countryside in 1970' Conference which was in direct line of succession from 1963's National Nature Week. But it very much broadened the field. Till then conservation had largely meant nature conservation. But from 1965 onwards it involved the countryside and everything in it. Market towns, villages, farms, historic buildings, ancient monuments, places of scenic beauty, rivers, lakes, forests, mountains—all were looked at with a view to conserving their features or eliminating whatever disfigured them. We heard more and more about the quality and the problems of life in the countryside. In one of my diaries I suggested that if rural mid Wales was to go on being habitable at all then it must be given a rest from being a mock battleground for military jets. Since then another decade or so has gone by and still we have these ever more terrifying planes screaming past just overhead. Their effect is overwhelming; sometimes the noise hits straight into the brain and it is all you can do not to throw yourself down in panic. You protest of course. You write off to officialdom and get a letter back from someone in the Arcadian peace of White-hall, someone who presumably has never experienced the noise of a jet screaming right inside his head. He rather tetchily suggests that you are exaggerating and that in fact these planes are far higher than you think. (Very comforting, this.) But, he adds considerately, if you do see an aircraft you think is flying below the allowed limit, you have only to report its number to the authorities and your complaint will be investigated. You feel like writing back to ask how one takes the number of an aircraft that flashes by just over your head at 600 miles an hour. But what's the use? These abominations will be with us until sufficient public pressure is aroused against them. But in a thinly populated region like ours protest is bound to be weak. So we shall, I fear, continue to be a persecuted minority.

Like the poet, from the troubles of this world I turn to ducks: and in the spring it is shelducks. In late March 1965, I described how good it is to see the shelducks come circling over Ynys Edwin fields on their first fly-round of the season. All winter they belong very strictly to the mud-flats. Then suddenly one day after mid March their internal clocks strike some sacred hour and these sea-loving fowl rise off the estuary and come flying over to the woods. It may be a move of not more than three hundred yards but it is quite as definite an act of migration as the wheatear's three thousand miles. The difference is that the shelducks' first visit to the woods may last only a few minutes and then they go straight back to the estuary. Next morning they come again and stay a bit longer and this process of gradual acclimatization goes on for weeks. It is, after all, a great upheaval for them after three-quarters of a year in the open light of the shore to find themselves living in the green twilight of the woods among a lot of birds and animals they are not used to. But they survive all right, these large, black, white and chestnut birds that look half-duck, half-goose. And every March we are grateful to see them flying just over the house, the ducks quacking, the drakes whistling, to tell us it is spring again even if east winds still blow and snow drifts lie under the hedges.

Early in 1966 one of my diaries welcomed the news that in North America there were reported to be four times as many bird-watchers as wildfowlers. In other words: for every American for whom it was a joy to see a bird drop dead from the sky, there were four who would prefer to see the bird fly on. I hoped that this was true of Britain too and suggested that the time might come when as well as hunting, shooting and fishing rights, we might have bird-watching and natural history rights; and that some landowners might find it would pay them better to allow access to naturalists' trusts than to blood sports interests. Also the naturalists would probably take a more active part in the conservation of an estate than any shooting syndicate would. Though so far there is little evidence of such a revolutionary change taking place, I still feel it must come in due course.

That summer I wrote about umbellifers and how man reacts to the many different species. Some he fears: such as the evil-smelling hemlock with ominous purple-spotted stem. Some he hates: especially the ground elder which year after year defeats him in the perennial border. Some uplift his heart: the beautiful cow parsley, pignut and burnet saxifrage. Some he finds good for dosing himself with or for flavouring his food: fennel, parsley, spignel, sweet cicely, lovage, caraway, coriander, angelica, dill. Some, like parsnip and carrot, he wolfs down in quantity. But though he welcomes many into the kitchen garden, who, I asked, could blame him for not wanting many of these elbowing umbellifers in his flower garden? This led on to the giant hogweeds that we had planted in our garden at Ynys Edwin the previous year and which were now ten feet tall and still going up. Next week educating letters began to arrive. 'I am writing to warn you that this plant can be very dangerous' was typical of most of them. Children all over the country, it seemed, were coming up in huge blisters as a result of breaking off sticks or leaves of hogweed to play with and getting the acrid juices on their skin, especially in bright sunlight. I was grateful for all these thoughtful hogweedy letters. They ended with one from a man who said he was experimenting with eating giant hogweed. From him I never heard again.

Air-gun manufacturers would not have welcomed my diary for 10 December 1966. In it I sent seasonal best wishes to all parents who resisted little Willie's plea that he be given an air-gun for Christmas. Air-guns, I said, might be all right if used only on proper targets but they seldom are. We all know what happens; sooner or later, they are used against sparrows, starlings, blackbirds, thrushes and other birds of garden and hedgerow. Few of these victims are shot cleanly. Most are injured and die slowly. To buy little Willie an air-gun, I reckoned, was to start him off on the wrong foot. As he gets older his little air-gun becomes a despised toy and he goes and buys himself a more powerful one. Then he ventures deeper into the countryside and does greater damage to wildlife. In a countryside in which more guns are firing than ever before in history it seems time that a beginning be made to reduce their number. Not that I blame little Willie for wanting a gun. He is conditioned from an early age into the notion that firing a gun is a manly form of behaviour. Anyway, who can censure him for eventually going in for blood sports when he has before him the example of some of the Very Best People for ever murdering grouse and pheasants for amusement?

The year 1967 was not very old before conservationists lost a hard and expensively fought battle. The House of Lords finally agreed to the construction of a reservoir in upper Teesdale though they knew full well that it would destroy a unique habitat for rare plants. All the same, many people, conservationists among them, felt that this defeat was not undeserved. After all, if this was such a botanically precious site why had it not been made a nature reserve years before? One thing that came out strongly from this dispute was how totally ignorant the promoters of this reservoir were about the natural fauna and flora of Britain and why they should be conserved. As I mentioned in my diary of 14 January, when a top-ranking I.C.I. scientist was interviewed on the radio he seemed quite pathetically bewildered by the massive support the botanists had been able to muster in defence of 'a few violets', as he put it. Surely, there must be something deeply wrong with our educational system if it produces highly trained people so totally unaware of any values outside those of their own narrow specialized grooves?

Still, the Teesdale campaign was not wholly wasted. It put conservationists a little more on their toes. And I'm sure it taught the general public that there really was a strong body of opinion concerned about the future of British wild animals and plants. It certainly became easier after that to talk to people about conservation. As when I called on a Welsh hill-farmer with an offer (from the West Wales Naturalists' Trust) to buy a peat bog that had some rare plants in it. As I looked at this rugged old sheep man whose face looked as hard as the grey rocks all round I wondered how long it would take for my proposition to be grasped by a mind which, though keenly alert to matters concerning farming, the chapel and local politics, might never have entertained an idea such as conservation. I needn't have doubted. Though a few years, or even a few months before, an approach like this would have been received with incomprehension or even suspicion, times had changed. Thanks to all the Teesdale publicity he knew all about botanists and their interests and was quite prepared to talk about conserving his patch of bog.

That year I pleaded for the frog. I had seen a buzzard taking frogs from a pool. That was legitimate predation. But what many people were beginning to feel was not at all legitimate was the predation that goes on in order to provide frogs for biology students to dissect. I was able to quote the Professor of Zoology at Oxford who in *Oryx*, the journal of the Fauna Preservation Society, had written a strong attack on the 'uncontrolled exploitation of a species of animal or plant for research and teaching purposes'. 'In our efforts to teach biology to our students in schools and universities,' said the Professor, 'we have now almost eliminated the common frog from the fauna of the British Isles. We have depleted the fauna of the sea round marine biological stations to the point where irreversible changes may have been caused in the natural environment.' Perhaps these were over-statements (the frog, for instance, is still abundant in wilder places) but they were an indication of a parlous state of affairs.

January 1968 found me deploring the industrialization of Anglesey. A nuclear power-station built on a hitherto unspoiled headland was being followed by a huge aluminium smelter at Holyhead. My remarks brought a very disagreeable letter from one reader. He was entitled to his opinion and if he wished to waste his time writing crotchety letters, that was up to him. One thing he said, however, has stuck in my mind: he disliked the trend he detected in all the Country Diarists (thank Heaven we were all in the dock together), to 'meddle in politics'. He went on: 'I am sure of one thing—I and thousands of others who read "Country Diary" do not go to it for politics.' Up to a point I could sympa-thize with him. I like to get away from politics too. But, I asked, could any country writer with the slightest awareness of reality just go on babbling o' green fields and kidding his readers that all was well in those fields?

Unrepentant, my diaries continued to 'meddle in politics'. Near to Machynlleth a narrow lane branches off a main road up a side valley well known for its beauty. It winds and climbs over a hill, then drops through woods into the deep cleft of the gorge. There are gates across the road at intervals; and there are places where river and lane are squeezed together by rocky walls and cars can-not pass each other. Then one day in 1968 we were astonished to find that a signpost saying 'Scenic Route' and pointing up this lane, had been erected on the main road. It was easy to see how such an absurdity had been perpetrated. Somebody sits planning in an office a hundred miles away and soon a whole crowd of motorists are battling with each other in a lane so restricted that the only sensible notice-board for it would have been 'Unsuitable for Motors'. A few years have gone since then. The 'Scenic Route' notice has disappeared. And just as cars are being restricted in the centres of cities so it is beginning to be accepted that cars are incompatible with the beauty and enjoyment of narrow, peaceful valleys. Of mountains, too, I hope, because 1968 brought another road proposal I couldn't let by without a protest. This new route (we have heard little about it lately but doubtless we shall) was to loop round Plynlimon at a high level and so become a panoramic route for motorists. It would also destroy yet another of the few mountain solitudes now left in southern Britain. My argument was that the car already has access to so many parts of the uplands that the last wildernesses should now be left for the enjoyment of present and future generations of hill-walkers who want to get away from engines of all sorts whether on cars, Land-Rovers, tractors, power-boats or Hovercraft.

In September that year I wrote in praise of golf-courses. A friend had phoned to say that while playing a round on one of our local links he had found a patch of 140 autumn lady's tresses. In June he had seen fifty-eight bee-orchids on the same course. Farther up the coast other links were rich with marsh orchids, pyramidal orchids and even had a little of the rare maiden pink. Golf, to those who don't play it, can seem a very strange occupation—walking along and earnestly giving a little white ball a knock with a stick from time to time. But conservationists can only be grateful for the golf-mania. For although the greens and other lawn-like stretches may be botanical deserts, the rough is often full of treasures. Undoubtedly, were it not for the golf courses along the Cardigan Bay coast, the dunes they occupy would now be built-up areas or caravan sites.

In May 1969, I was faintly optimistic about the future of the red kite. Under protection it had doubled its population in ten years to a couple of dozen pairs. Given another decade it might, I said, achieve fifty pairs and be spreading from Wales into England. But kites wouldn't get very far into the lowlands of England until gamekeepers and others ceased to harass them. In most of England, in contrast to most of Wales, there are too many guns and traps in use against 'vermin' to give much hope for the larger birds of prey. So for the time being we should look on Wales as a bird-bank holding considerable assets. Let us continue to protect these valuable Welsh stocks. For the time must surely come when the average English sportsman's attitude to predators will change and will allow magnificent creatures like kites and harriers to resume their rightful place throughout the British countryside.

Royal visits to Snowdonia being topical in 1969, the year of the investiture of the Prince of Wales, I was pleased to revive the memory in my diary of a long-forgotten royal visitor of the summer of 1844. This was the King of Saxony who, with his retinue, climbed Snowdon (and thereby became the first royal person of modern times to do so?). Unfortunately he struck a bad day; but the summit was not without welcome, as one of his followers related: 'We found refuge in a small wooden shed erected for the protection of travellers from the rain and the wind, in which the host kept up a welcome fire. The man presently prepared a singular brown mixture which he sold for coffee and furnished some greyish oatmeal cake as an accompaniment. There were no spirituous liquors to be had because the occupier, with no small degree of self-satisfaction, gave us to understand that his wooden hut was to be regarded as a temperance inn.'

In July 1969 a generous friend took me off to visit Tsavo, Serengeti and other East African parks. The quick tour of the great wildlife reserves had become enormously popular, especially among Americans and West Germans. And now more British and other nationalities were joining these well-organized safaris into wildernesses which, until not so long ago, were reachable only by tough adventurers. With the game-park hotels booked up the whole year round, tourism was booming and the future for wildlife conservation looked bright: as long as the game parks continued to bring in foreign money they could be justified by those who had to argue with the increasing numbers of Africans who felt strongly that animals should not be given priority over people and that a better use for the parks would be as cattle ranges. Not that conservationists could be entirely happy about the situation. The trans-world tourism that was bringing the money to the parks was also using vast quantities of aeroplane fuel: so that in saving one natural resource, wildlife, we were depleting another, oil. And when we reached the point at which oil got scarce, what hope for African wildlife then?

Still, there was good hope for wildlife in Britain in 1969. The R.S.P.B. was expanding its work and had launched an appeal for funds to buy four new reserves and this money was eventually subscribed. As I wrote in my diary, I think many people support this sort of appeal not because they are especially concerned about birds so much as about the places where the birds live. There is a wilderness-loving side to human nature, a trait that gets stronger perhaps the more we are urbanized. And money is subscribed so that old estates, woods and marshes may go on surviving unspoilt. It gives people strength and happiness to feel that they can go and visit a nature reserve once in a while, as a butterfly sips briefly at a flower. Readers have written to me saying that what 'A Country Diary' gives them more than anything is an assurance that while they are at work in city office, factory or house, the world of nature is still going on 'out there' and that efforts are being made to ensure that it shall continue.

I think that 1970 was a suitable year in which to bring these chronicles to a close. It saw the culmination of a campaign that had its origins back in National Nature Week 1963. Then we had the 'Countryside in 1970' Conference. And in 1970 we were caught up in European Conservation Year. This was a movement that had its detractors, of course. European 'Conversation' Year, they sneeringly called it. But that is exactly what it was meant to be. It got people talking, as they had never talked before, about our environmental problems, problems that are going to take not a Conservation Year but a Conservation Century to put right. A wildlife problem I wanted to see put right was the international trade in animals and birds for the pet trade. Moroccan tortoises, for instance, of which Britain alone imports 300,000 a year, most of which die in the first or second winter here. As for the cage-bird industry—this is a disgrace second to none. We in Britain protect most of our birds very well but are hypocritical enough to take advantage of the fact that other countries fail to protect theirs: so we allow our cage-bird industry to import thousands annually, the catching and shipping of which, incidentally, cause innumerable deaths.

In fact, 1970 began rather well. In a January diary I was able to celebrate that the large-scale use of D.D.T. in Britain seemed to be on its way out. If it had conquered malaria in some places then all credit to it. But now that we had non-persistent insecticides to do the job we need not shed tears over D.D.T. and other substances that had in recent years been showered wholesale on fields and forests, poisoning everything within range, to be then washed into rivers where they killed fish and the predators of fish, and so down to the sea until the farthest limits of the ocean were now polluted. What concerned me was the degree of pollution people were prepared to accept. Lake Erie, 10,000 square miles of it, was almost dead. Yet apparently the people who live by it accepted its death as an inevitable part of progress. It was the champions of progress in the nineteenth century who convinced the western world that it was heading to 'its manifest destiny'. And in the twentieth century, until very recently, they convinced most people that all scientific and technological progress was good for us. From Thoreau onwards dissenting voices were few. Of his contemporaries he said: 'They may go their way to their manifest destiny which I trust is not mine.' But by 1970 the world was full of Thoreaus. People everywhere were talking of pollution. Only politicians and businessmen were still talking of progress. Though now they called it 'growth'.

In this part of Wales the drama of 1970 was that here we were in Conservation Year and along comes Rio Tinto Zinc with monstrous proposals to extract gold from the incomparably beautiful estuary of the Mawddach and to open a huge open-cast mine for low-grade copper ore on the slopes of Rhobell Fawr, both areas being in the Snowdonia National Park. It was known, too, that other companies were waiting in the wings to see how R.T.Z. got on with their attempt. But European Conservation Year was a bad year to come forward with such vandalistic schemes. For though the Government were generally in favour of mineral exploitation, the conservationists were able to quote the Prime Minister, Mr. Edward Heath, as saying: 'The protection of our countryside and the prevention of pollution are among the highest priorities of the seventies.' Ultimately, as we all know, R.T.Z. withdrew its Snowdonia schemes. But I doubt if many of us, though relieved, felt much like celebrating. The affair had shown how vulnerable are even the most cherished areas of

Britain. We know that such threats could recur at any time and the wearying struggle would start all over again. Prospectors haunt the hills of Snowdonia still.

That year I wrote several diaries attacking the mining proposals. Not all were published. I was 'meddling in politics' again and this time it was the features editor who did not approve. 'I am afraid', he wrote, 'that in spite of its topical note it has always been our policy to keep political ramification out of this essentially pastoral column.' Essentially pastoral, so that's what we diarists were supposed to be! Why hadn't they told us right from the start that all they wanted was nymphs and shepherds, agricultural shows and the first cuckoo of spring? I did not reply to the features editor because I knew he was only carrying out orders. The editor himself had phoned me that he had received a complaint about a previous diary of mine from someone very high up in R.T.Z. So big business tries to stifle the press. Still it was interesting to learn that R.T.Z. was getting so sensitive to public opinion as to feel it worthwhile trying to silence even us poor country diarists.

In our county of Cardigan (it had not yet reverted to its ancient name of Ceredigion) we celebrated European Conservation Year by making an inventory of what we called our 'treasures'. Through my diaries I was able to give a few progress reports on this particular exercise—how, throughout the villages and hamlets (mainly through great work done by the Women's Institutes), there were innumerable talks, films and exhibitions, all promoting the idea of conservation. The chief message was that we needed to look with vigilant eyes at our countryside. Long-accepted eyesores were to be accepted no longer. And things that were really good—our treasures—had to be cherished and protected. It was all a fascinating experience, going round talking to people, often in remote villages, and hearing about everything they particularly valued in their parish—it might be a church, a farmhouse, a mill, a pool, a wood, a waterfall, a patch of wildflowers, a viewpoint —anything that gave delight. Unexpected discoveries too, like the farm outbuilding that, on examination, was found to be a fine, late medieval barn. But the really valuable part of the operation

F

was the stirring in people of a new consciousness of their surroundings. For this is the beginning of true conservation.

To end with, let me go back to 1966. That was the year when the country diarists emerged at last from the obscurity of being mere initials. On Saturday 30 April, I had to answer to my full name for the first time. And that day the *Guardian* published an article about us by Geoffrey Moorhouse who concluded by saying: 'The contributors to "A Country Diary" are not just keeping track of what goes on "out there" among the grass roots. They are, in their own way, manning one of the weakening frontiers of our lifeline.' If he were writing that article today could he still say the frontier is weakening? I suppose he could. But I feel that there is now a greater awareness of the world's plight than there was then and a greater desire to do something about it. People truly are beginning to have doubts about continuous economic growth. The need to conserve our resources by recycling is at last being recognized. Pollution really is being tackled on some fronts though by no means all. If the rivers of the seventies are cleaner than those of the sixties and the air of towns safer to breathe then there is hope yet for the rest of the century.

👾 5. Spring Idyll in Clare

Perhaps, when we went one spring to the west of Ireland, it was because I was hearing the call of ancestral voices, for mine is an Irish name. Also just then I was particularly occupied with Edward Lhuyd. For some time I had been fossicking around the Welsh mountains trying to find the plants he had discovered there in the late seventeenth century. (How fascinating that they should still be growing in the same localities after nearly three hundred years.) Then I read that Lhuyd had also been a botanical pioneer in Ireland, being the first recorder there (1699) of maidenhair fern, shrubby cinquefoil, Irish sandwort, kidney saxifrage and St. Dabeoc's heath. (What more delightful a quintet of plants could a botanist wish to have to his credit?) But Lhuyd really went to Ireland not to see plants but to see Ireland itself, Ireland as a major piece of the fragmented Celtic world about which he was planning to write his encyclopedia. I suppose it is an itch that comes to many in Wales at some time in their lives, this curiosity about another Celtic land across the water. It was something I had particularly felt ever since, one evening from the hill on Bardsey Island, I had looked across the sea through my binoculars and had seen three shapely Wicklow heights called Kippure, Mullaghcleevaun and Lugnaquillia outlined black against a fiery sky.

We went with fellow naturalists Cecil Lambourne and his wife Jonny who have a great enthusiasm for wild places and are well-known campaigners for conservation. Having read several books by Robert Lloyd Praeger, who was Ireland's most distinguished writer on nature, we decided not to spread our short holiday thinly over a tour of the whole country but to concentrate on one locality. And since Praeger, though quivering with emotion about almost every square yard of Ireland, really overflowed about a district called the Burren, it was to the hills of Burren we went. Who, after all, could resist such lines as: 'He who has viewed the thousands of acres of this arctic-alpine plant [mountain avens] in full flower on the limestones of the Burren, from hilltop down to sea-level, has seen one of the loveliest sights that Ireland has to offer the botanist'? Thousands of acres! On Snowdonia's mountain ledges we had sought and eventually found tiny relict patches of this avens. We had found it in fair quantity in the Alps. We knew it grew widely in the wastes of the arctic tundra. And this made us the more curious to see such a tough mountaineer, such an ice-resisting northerner, luxuriating in mildness and soft rain in County Clare.

We motored from Rosslare westwards across Ireland, through mile upon mile of level pastures and hedges, an experience of greenness that does nothing to prepare you for what is to come as you near the Atlantic. Somewhere in Clare the land begins to roll until at last you reach a crest with a far view ahead and there before you lies a region of blunt-topped hills that would be totally unimpressive if they were green but which, because they rise naked and white above the world, make such a striking landscape you immediately want to photograph or sketch or write home about it. Twenty minutes later you are in this pallid land, the rocky slopes rising away on each side to distant ridge tops, and you begin to realize how extensive all this limestone is.

The size of the place is indeed one of its biggest surprises. The more you listen to people rhapsodizing about the carpets of flowers on the slopes of Black Head (where most of them go to see the Burren flora) the more your idea of the Burren gets narrowed to one small spread of limestone tilted above the sea. Not until you get into the heart of the region and climb to one of the summits and see all round you other gaunt, bare hills undulating into the distance do you realize that here is an outcrop of carboniferous limestone that must cover at least fifty square miles. And it all looks so incredibly dry after the verdant Ireland you have just left behind. Here you are, in the Irish far west, where your friends back home have all warned you it rains six days in seven, and you find a land as arid-looking as the mountains of Afghanistan.

First impressions can deceive. You go a few miles on and the bare rock ends. You find long stretches of the roadside where there is a mean soil covered by a thin but flowery turf. There are even areas dense with hazel scrub. And in a few sheltered valleys there is real soil that produces trees of full stature as well as a farm or two. But apart from these scattered holdings this is virtually a land without people except round its edges. And largely without water. For the copious rain quickly vanishes down countless crevices into underground streams that flow along measureless caverns to the sea.

At a distance this country might seem botanically hopeless unless you are familiar with the similar limestone hills of northern England and know that you need only to look into the cracks (in Yorkshire they are 'grikes') that everywhere fissure the grey-white rock to find all the plants you have come to seek. Down in these crevices they all grow very happily, rooted as they are in rich humus and never-failing moisture. There they are safe from two of plant life's worst enemies—grazing animals and desiccating winds.

In all the rich Burren flora there are, I think, four species more memorable than the rest, not for rarity (only one is rare) but for being so delightfully abundant. There is mountain avens which decorates crannies and riots down slopes almost everywhere you go. Even when its white rose-like flowers are over it is still completely endearing for its glossy little oaken leaves and its delicately spiralled seed-heads that later fluff out into white cottony fruits. Almost as striking is the early purple orchid. Though this is a common orchid in many other parts of Britain I doubt if it flourishes anywhere more abundantly than here in the Burren. Everywhere it springs from the open turf, shines dark or pale in rock shadows, meets you at eye-level on wall tops, bends to the wind of the hills, adds colour—purple, pink or white—all down the slopes to the tide. Even so this orchid is not the showiest plant of the Burren. Wherever you wander it is outshone by the blood-red cranesbill that sits opulent in clefts and basins and tumbles joyous over rocks and ledges. Then the fourth of my quartet of colour-makers is the rare (but not rare here) spring gentian whose stars are locally so crowded they make whole patches of ground intensely blue.

There are other choice species. The dense-flowered orchid, for instance, which at first you despair of finding until you get your eye in, by which time you realize it is in fact not at all uncommon but merely nondescript, a short green spike of crowded fat seedpods lost in the short green grass, its dingy flowers so minute you wonder what possible use they can be to the plant. Still one rejoices to see such a singular orchid in its only corner of the British Isles. It is one of the Burren's mystery species. It belongs rather to the Mediterranean world—Morocco, Spain, Greece—and why it and several other plants from down there should find themselves on the Irish side of the ocean is one of those problems which botanogeographers (if there is such a word) love to play with but do not always solve.

A far better looking rarity is *Saxifraga rosacea*. Easily overlooked because its white flowers are so like those of the common mossy saxifrage, it is distinguished by its cushions being neater and its leaf-rosettes often red. The slopes below Black Head are one of its stations: there it grows in fair plenty down to a few feet above the heaving green seas, enjoying the spray of the thrift zone. A fellow rarity, but much more easily found, is the hoary rock-rose whose pale yellow little flowers you may well have confused in other places with those of the common rock-rose: for where the two grow together they often hybridize and produce a bewildering range of progeny. But in the Burren there are no such hazards. Here, despite all the heavenly limestone that looks so perfect for it, the common rock-rose is absent. And it is as astonishingly lacking throughout almost the whole of Ireland.

Go in mid May to the Burren if you want to catch spring gentian and dense-flowered orchid in flower and find the avens still at its best. Even early June is leaving things late if the year is a forward one. But June brings splendours May knows little about —vast numbers of fly orchids, for instance. July, too, has its delights, outstandingly the dark red helleborines which, especially on the higher rocks, can be counted in their hundreds. And near the village of Ballyvaughan and in several other places there are acres of shrubby cinquefoil, a yellow-flowered beauty extremely local in the British Isles but in the Burren burned like gorse to get rid of it. It grows best in the damp ground of valley bottoms, well away from bare rock.

Rarities are only a part of the fascination of the Burren's flora. This limestone with its feet in the Atlantic is kind to a whole world of common species that add enormously to the show. Everywhere birdsfoot trefoil makes deep yellow splashes. Burnet rose, the chief wild rose of the Burren, has flowers here that are not all the usual white: some are of a lovely deep apricot you will rarely see elsewhere. There are stands of white moon daisies of wondrous luxuriance. Thyme, yellow wort, mountain everlasting, primrose, eyebright, vernal sandwort, scurvy grass, herb robert—these are delightful not only because so abundant but because so obviously contented and flowering so generously. The common daisy, sitting privately in a cup of white rock, becomes a compelling subject for your camera.

Then there are the crevice-growing trees. But better call them treelets, these typically Burren ashes, hollies, buckthorns whose feet are six or eight feet down in the grikes and whose heads just reach up to the level of the limestone, peep out but venture no higher because compelled to spread horizontally along the grike. On seaward slopes it is the wind, the salty wind burning off their growing points that makes them cringe. Elsewhere it is browsing animals (no shortage of goats on these rocky slopes) that keep them down. Yet though the trees look so strange down there in their cracks there is nothing really amiss with them for their leaves shine with good health. In the Burren you find that the junipers also have opted for horizontality, growing not down in fissures but spreading like mats over many a yard of flat rock, the way mountain junipers grow.

Ferns, of course, are totally in their element in the deep moist fissures of this frost-free land of the Burren. Not surprisingly the tender maidenhair is more abundant here than anywhere in the British Isles: more magnificent, too, its fronds reaching two feet long. On the slopes of the highest hill, Slieve Elva (1,134 feet), you will find it up to little short of the summit. It is also abundant on the Arans which are islands of limestone some miles off-shore and have a Burren-style flora. No one will be surprised to learn that the lime-loving hartstongue is about the commonest fern of the Burren: crevices yards long and feet wide are solid with its magnificent fronds. And if you have only known rusty-back as a fern of lime-mortared walls you will look at it with new eyes when you see it anchored in the living rock from end to end of the Burren. Wall rue, brittle bladder fern, common spleenwort and hard shieldfern: these grow in splendour through all the land, some I daresay throwing up unusual forms that excite serious fernseekers.

Eventually, after two or three days of ecstatic botanizing on the Burren your superlatives are all exhausted and you begin to look at the place more calmly. You now get your ecological eye in focus and think in terms of the total flora instead of individual species. So next time you clamber up the slopes near Black Head it dawns on you that the vegetation rises up the slopes in distinct zones; and also that, despite the whole area being of limestone, one of the most pronounced of these zones is a bracken one, that another is of bearberry and yet a third is pure heather—all species that are most determined lime-haters. But this is quite as it should be. For though it's true you are in Clare where life may even yet be strange and fay, yet the ecology is straightforward enough. In districts of unstinted rainfall the passing centuries may wash the liminess even out of limestone, leaving a surface humus as acid as the granitic top of Cadair Idris or the lavas of Crib Goch.

Carn Sefin is a good hill to climb if you have two hours to spare at Black Head (which I hardly need tell you is as white as the rest of the scenery—the whiteness coming more, it seemed to me, from the pallor of the lichens than from that of the rock itself). On Carn Sefin you go easily up the gentle slope, always provided you watch out for those toe-catching crannies. You scramble up a little cliff and on you go up another mildly sloping shelf. In a few hundred yards another little cliff and so on and up you go, always thinking the next ridge is the top. But at last you find the summit cairn and look around at the great scene of coast and ocean that has built up behind: the three Aran Islands one beyond the other in the west; below you the blue spread of Galway Bay with all its inlets and its islets; then in the north, across the water, fair Connemara, land of rocks and peat bogs, rising to the far-off Twelve Bens.

On this bare hill of Carn Sefin you will find very little animal life. But especially lower down you may see choice butterflies like chalk-hill blue, dark green fritillary and (though far from any woods) the delicate little wood white. And there is one moth—I have not seen it—called the Burren green, found here but no-where else in the British Isles. Birds are few on the tops—only flitting pipits and a skylark or two. But near the sea genuine, wild rock-doves race along the cliffs, their grey wings black-banded, their rumps pure white. White terns and whiter gannets plop into deep green water. If you wait long enough you will see black guillemots swim by and glimpse the surprising redness of their feet as they dive into the translucent water. Though this is the Atlantic the seals that lie on the sand at low tide off Ballyvaughan are not Atlantic grey seals but the smaller, common seal which here has one of its local Irish colonies.

Down the coast south from Black Head you lose the Burren altogether in quite a few miles. As you quit the limestone the vegetation, the whole feel of the place, changes. You are now in a land of sandstones that turn a gritty face to the west and rise straight up from the ocean for nearly seven hundred feet to form the famous Cliffs of Moher on whose ledges you will find a multitudinous seabird colony, thousands of shrieking, caterwaul-ing, groaning kittiwakes, herring gulls, guillemots, razorbills, shags and puffins. Look out for choughs just here. They often perch on O'Brien's Tower, a viewpoint near the cliff edge. Near by is a car park and often flocks of holiday makers. But come hooting cars, shouting children, transistor radios—the choughs accept them all with nonchalance.

The hotel centre of the Burren is Lisdoonvarna. Here come the tourists who wish to explore the terraced hills; the cavers whose ambition is to see them from underneath; and the valetudinarians who drink the sulphurous water for their various ailments. I shall remember Lisdoonvarna for a violet curtain that spread for yards across a dripping natural wall overhanging a shadowed stream: it was a massed colony of giant butterworts, one of Ireland's loveliest plants, and here all the more wonderful for being arranged vertically and at eye level in a world of rock and moss, green gloom and musical water.

The road north from Lisdoonvarna to Ballyvaughan takes you right across the high-level limestones. But these uplands are not the whole of the Burren. Go away south-east, leave the hills altogether and you come to a different region but one that in its way is just as unique. The fissured limestone goes on but it continues now as a plain of skeletal white rock that cradles a group of small lakes. The plants of the higher slopes are nearly all down here too. And there are others which prefer the damper climate the lakes create: the marsh orchids for which the west of Ireland is famous; the elegant meadow thistle; northern bedstraw and lesser meadow-rue looking unusually prosperous; the rare and lovely fen violet straggling up to two feet tall where it can lean on the stiffer stems of bog rush. There are more trees in these lowlands but, as on the hills, many have to be content with fissure life: spindle, guelder rose, hawthorn and all the rest have to be sought for in their pavement slots.

As you wander through this land of pale-faced rock or poor thin turf, enjoying the glint of sun on lake, towers that stand against the skyline, the geometrical shapes of the hills, here and there you will find yourself gazing inquiringly into green basins in the ground, some only a few feet deep and a few yards across, others many yards deep and hundreds of yards across. They look as if they ought to be lakes, these curious depressions. But they are not for the simple reason they all have a sink-hole in the bottom down which the rain drains either quickly or slowly away, but usually only in the summer or in some other dry spell. Go in winter or after a few days of heavy rain in summer and you will find that many of these hollows have become lakes and will remain lakes as long as there is plenty of rain. Not that they fill from the top. It is from the bottom, up the plug-hole, that the water comes. For these strange hollows—they are called turloughs (pronounced 'turlochs')—sit above underground streams. And just as surface rivers swell in flood and overbrim their banks, so the underground streams of the Burren rise up from below and fill their turloughs. Low-lying turloughs may even be linked underground with the sea. Praeger described a turlough near Coole whose level varied with the ebb and flow of tides three miles away.

Each turlough (the word means 'dry lake') is an individual. So much depends on the gauge of the plug-hole, the size of the stream below and how far down it is. There are turloughs that always have at least some water in the bottom. Others flood and empty very quickly. Some may remain as lakes half the year or more. All confront plant life with serious survival problems. The average marsh plant does not take to the erratic life of turloughs: it needs water ever gently seeping past its roots. Real aquatic plants could never survive the turlough's dry spells. Nor could many dry-ground plants endure the immersions. So what are we left with? The most obvious turlough successes are semi-aquatic mosses that spread a dark green or blackish mat in the deepest hollows, giving them a really sinister look. (Local people avoid a turlough as they would the crater of a volcano.) Then up the slopes of the turlough the vegetation is zoned according to the amount of immersion it can bear. Of flowering plants one of the very happiest is that yellow potentilla of roadsides and damp ground, the silverweed: in many turloughs it is a thick-piled carpet. Another success is common (not marsh) birdsfoot trefoil. Fen violet is often there too. But all these are likely to be crowded out in the upper levels by a jungle of creeping willow, stone bramble, hawthorn, blackthorn and both alder and purging buckthorns.

In this land of lough and turlough there are other fascinations. One charming lake, Lough Bunny, has, besides tufted ducks, grebes and mergansers, an island with tall trees whose tops house what must be rare: a mixed breeding colony of herons and cormorants, just a few nests of each. And for lovers of past things there are, often ominous on the skyline, the great stone towers that are relics of the grey side of life in this often strife-torn land. Yeats enthusiasts will think here of the tower that stands tall in several of his poems, his tower of Ballylee, for Gort is in this land and not very far away stood the house of Coole among the seven woods by the lake where the wild swans came. There are far older buildings: medieval churches and monasteries in which Ireland is so rich; Dark Age and Iron Age forts set gaunt and watchful on the hills; hut remains perhaps of the Bronze Age; and going right back to the Neolithic time some quite perfect chambered tombs.

Without question this land of the Burren is one of the most unusual, one of the most interesting districts in western Europe. And because so sparsely inhabited it is still intact, still there in almost its pristine perfection. But for how much longer if the exploiters get hold of it, the tourism promoters, the hotel builders, the property speculators, the chalet and holiday-camp operators? Already a few holiday homes have been erected. And there is talk of a motorway that will whizz people in no time at all from Dublin to Galway. What hope for the Burren then unless it is carefully protected? I don't mean the declaring of a few nature reserves to safeguard selected samples of the flora. I mean some far greater, more imaginative act of conservation that would save the whole precious region from being vandalized by developers.

6. Tick-hunting in Andalusia

When Thoreau withdrew from society to live in his hut in Walden Woods his solitude was often disturbed by callers. But only in the warm season. In winter he was left almost entirely alone with the trees, the few birds, the frozen pond, and the deep Massachusetts snow. Then he was visited only by the most devoted and determined such as his friend who was a poet: 'The one who came from farthest to my lodge, through deepest snows and most dismal tempests, was a poet. A farmer, a hunter, a soldier, a reporter, even a philosopher, may be daunted; but nothing can deter a poet, for he is actuated by pure love. Who can predict his comings and goings? His business calls him out at all hours, even when doctors sleep.'

Penny and I felt like that when, before we came to Ynys Edwin, we were living not far away in a little hillside cottage called Felin-y-cwm, a mile up the narrow, wooded valley of the Einion stream. On winter nights we, like Thoreau, were tucked up 'as snug as a meadow mouse' and seldom had visitors. Yet through the darkness, sometimes trudging through snow drifts, there was one who came up over the mountain track and down to our door. And he, as if to give truth to Thoreau's words, was a poet. R. S. Thomas, then vicar of our parish, came to chat about many things: but above all about wild birds. For they are a very special part of his life.

Now poets, the good ones, occasionally get literary prizes. And it happened one day that R. S. Thomas was granted a bursary that carried with it the condition that it had to be spent on foreign travel, the idea being, I suppose, that visiting other countries broadens a writer's mind. But I fear that R. S. Thomas took a somewhat narrow view of what would broaden his: he saw it as an opportunity of adding to his life-list of birds. 'Tick-hunting' is what bird-watchers call it. You carry a card with a list of all the birds on it and you happily tick them off as you spot them. A fatuous occupation, you may say, but it gives people a lot of pleasure and is quite harmless unless, as sometimes happens, too many bird-watchers want to see the same rare bird and pursue it to the point of harassment.

On receiving his travel award R. S. Thomas resolved to go and see the birds of southern Spain. (He had been reading that inspiring book *Portrait of a Wilderness* by Guy Mountfort.) And he generously invited me to go with him as a passenger in his car. Because the grant was not enormous we would need to keep our expenses down by taking most of our food with us and by camping. So it came about that one morning in late April we set off for Andalusia.

As our ship began to move down the Solent from Southampton we began putting ticks on our cards. Herring gull, cormorant, oyster-catcher. . . . In mid-Channel a few more commoners. . . . In Cherbourg a crow and a starling. (Even the most soaring lists need these bread and butter species to get them off the ground.) The only choice birds we got that first day were a barn-owl and a nightingale, both heard over a frugal supper at our camp near Rennes. Next day, heeding only the call of the south, we drove across Brittany without stopping to look for birds. But by chance we got our first touch of glamour—a golden oriole near Saintes— before we camped on the Landes coast at Arachon. And there is nothing like the first golden oriole for putting northern bird-watchers in good spirits and convincing them that the golden age is beginning. No golden age for us next day, however. It was a day that should have carried us well into Spain but because of a Montagu's harrier and other events it did not. Heading south we saw a signpost on our right, 'La Route des Lacs', and what tick-hunter short of waterbirds could resist a lakeside road? So fate diverted us from the Bordeaux–San Sebastian highway into a quiet little coastal road that led with promise through open heathlands and scattered groves with an occasional hint of sand-dunes far on our right. It was then we saw our Montagu's harrier floating over the heather and we rejoiced, for this is a rare bird nearly everywhere. We stopped. Since this wild, apparently un-peopled land had harriers it probably had other good birds. So though we were going to fall behind our strict schedule we felt we must spare this Arcadia a little while. We got out and walked along the road. In a few minutes we had seen a Dartford warbler and had gazed enraptured up into a tree at our first Bonelli's warbler. Next moment we were being arrested by a French military officer for spying on a military base. (It was there all right, this base, but in the excitement we just hadn't spotted the rather small notice-boards.)

All that sunny morning we were interrogated by the comman-dant of this top-secret defence establishment; and then re-interrogated all afternoon by the civil police especially summoned from Bordeaux. It was an agonizing waste of our precious holiday. But it had its amusing moments. As when we were being ques-tioned outside the base headquarters soon after we arrived. Suddenly R. S. Thomas stepped out of the group and raised his field glasses to stare intently up into a tree. 'Woodchat shrike,' he said after a few moments. And taking out his bird-list he solemnly ticked it off. We spent the next ten minutes explaining to the military police what a bird-list is and what a woodchat shrike is and pointing to its picture in the book. How thankful we were to the *Field Guide* for giving us the French names of birds! All the same, anyone who thinks his French is good should try explaining the mysteries of bird-ticking to a group of suspicious French military police. To our captors this incident probably appeared a clever piece of acting and convinced them that we really were dangerous spies. Or maybe it just confirmed them in their belief that all the British are mad. Though the proceedings ended at last in handshakes and genial good-byes, one fact could not be altered: we had lost a whole precious day. That night we got no farther than a camping place by a pine-surrounded pool called Lac Léon, many miles short of where we had intended to be.

Next morning we entered Spain along the coast road and kept carefully to the main highway all the way to Burgos. Spanish military police, we decided, would be even more difficult to deal with than French ones. All that day, because we hardly ever stopped, we got only nine ticks on the list: but one was for a species new to us both, an evasive little bird that spluttered out an unfamiliar loud but cheerful phrase from a thicketed streamside and which we eventually identified as a Cetti's warbler. That was the day the corn buntings began. To us, coming from west Wales, a few corn buntings along the wires were a novelty at first. But when, down that long road to Burgos, we realized that there was a corn bunting on the wires every few hundred metres, they soon began to get tedious. There were plenty of wire-perching species we wanted to see—shrikes, chats, flycatchers—but no, practically every bird on the wires all that long day was a corn bunting. We had not dreamed there were so many in all the world.

It was from Burgos southward, and especially after Valladolid, that life began to change, that we felt we had crossed an invisible frontier. The early morning in our camp under tall poplars at Burgos gave us wrynecks laughing among the branches: and a wryneck is a good enough start to any British bird-watcher's day. In the same place serins chorused among the leaves and another valued tick went down for the spotless starling. We passed through Valladolid and Salamanca on a memorable day that soon gave us quail, little ringed plover and crested and short-toed larks. Overhead the first black kite came circling. And we felt we were getting into the real south when we began to see frequent hoopoes flapping across the road and scintillating bee-eaters perched along the wires. A red-roofed town with white storks on chimney pots and rows of lesser kestrels along the walls was for us a new species of town. We only needed a roller, we said, to convince us we really had reached southern Spain. And before we got to Salamanca we saw one, a joyous dazzle of blue as it dropped from a wire to snatch up a beetle off the ground. Soon afterwards a pure-white bird that came beating across the sky seemed an authentic touch of Africa—a cattle egret, a bird that lives in some numbers in Morocco and Algeria but has only the slenderest hold on Europe, mainly here in south Spain.

When you've reached far enough into Spain to tick off your first eighty birds you begin to find new species much harder to come by. But the trickle you do get are nearly all good quality. So on 1 May, still motoring on, we saw our first red kite gliding high over the road. Stopping awhile we heard the delicious song of a woodlark, now become so rare a sound in much of Britain. Among roadside birds was a small colony of great grey shrikes; farther on a black-eared wheatear; then one of Spain's most exclusive and beautiful species, the azure-winged magpie, seen briefly as it slipped away into a thicket.

So we came to Andalusia and to Seville, its chief city. On 2 May, however, there was a heat-wave. We could hardly breathe, there was an annihilating confusion of traffic and, of course, no birds. None, that is, except the swifts that arrowed back and forth across the burning sky and were presumably a mixture of common and pallid swifts, two species that are indistinguishable overhead. Thankfully we took the coast road from Seville towards Huelva along the north side of the Guadalquivir marshes, turning off at Almonte for El Rocio through scented plantations of pine and eucalyptus. The bridge at El Rocio, a place known to bird-watchers all over Europe, gave us squacco heron, night heron and little egret. Then we entered a different world—of wide sands and aromatic unfamiliar bushes and scattered trees—the strangely beautiful, wild world of the Coto Doñana, once a hunting reserve of the Dukes of Medina Sidonia but now a wildlife refuge, thanks to the World Wildlife Fund and the efforts of many private individuals.

Through all our five days on the Coto Doñana, which is in the hottest corner of Europe, the north African desert chose to breathe at us with a fiery breath. If it is like that at the beginning of May I never wish to go there in summer. Coolest places were the estuary marshes (called *marismas*) which stretch flatly away to an infinite horizon in the south. And the benign air of the *marismas* could be felt also in the heathy oak-scattered margins of the estuary: but the farther we wandered from the water the hotter it was. Still, the cork oaks shed a deep shade and escape from the sun was easy enough. It was seawards where the real heat lay in wait. For between the heathlands and the sea stretches one of the widest dune areas in Europe, mountainous ranges of sand going

G

away ridge beyond ridge towards the invisible Atlantic, as if a chunk of the Sahara has escaped across into Europe.

Though days were hot the nights were cool in our tents under tall, ancient gum trees. But to anyone thinking of camping in this region I would emphatically recommend a mosquito-proof tent if you want a night's sleep. True, Spain's mosquitoes are not malarial. But there is nothing else in their favour and there are millions of them. Yet though their tormenting keeps you awake there are compensations. Through the darkness across the *marismas* comes the 'oomp-oomp-oomp' of many bitterns; from the heathlands you hear the delicious wailing of the stone curlew and the 'tok-tok-tok' of red-necked nightjars; and in the trees overhead the passage of the night hours is registered by one of nature's machines, the Scops owl, which yelps its changeless 'kee-wick' every two seconds throughout the whole night, or so it seems. It is well to make the most of these noises because they come from birds very difficult to find by day. When you wake at dawn next morning to the song of the oriole and other splendid birds do not be over-hasty to shower ticks upon your card. For in the tops of those great gum-trees overhead roost several spotless starlings and the first thing they do when they wake is to practise their repertoire of imitations. Not that they need much practice. The average spotless starling is immaculate, if I may so put it, in his renderings of the songs and calls of orioles, curlews, wood sandpipers, redshanks and many others. It is all very confusing.

It was the *marismas* we looked at first. From a distance they seem a vast green plain but when you get to their edge you see they are shallow water, weedy with rushes and crowfoots. Everywhere there are birds flying. Whiskered terns, very lovely with their near-white wings and their pure-white cheeks and breasts, circle over their nesting colonies with rasping cries. Separate, but not far away, scores of black terns also wheel and chorus above their nests, their voices higher and more gentle than those of whiskered terns. Gull-billed terns, gleaming white and with distinctive black beaks, pass occasionally from remoter colonies. Everywhere are moorhens and common coots: but the crested coot, an African species that in Europe breeds only in south Spain, is far less easy to find. And you need to get close to it before you see the distinguishing red knobs on its head (they are often far less pronounced than those inflated, red balloons depicted by some bird artists).

In the midday heat the *marismas* were drying and retreating. Daily the margin of hardening mud grew wider and shore birds were beginning to nest. If we walked near the water there was constant harassment by angry stilts calling 'yik-yik-yik' as they flew over, trailing long drooping red legs behind their elegant black and white bodies. Pratincoles, too, were nesting there: they swooped about like small dark terns calling 'kirrit, kirrit'. On this same bare ground short-toed larks also had their nests. And always in the upper air there was a traffic of birds to and from their colonies in the cork oaks. Grey herons, spoonbills, egrets, sometimes a stork: out they flew to far feeding grounds in the *marismas* or flapped more heavily home. Occasionally marsh-harriers passed; and nearly always, somewhere in the sky, there were circling, diving and whinnying black kites.

The mixed heronries were incomparably beautiful. We could see them from far off, for the gleaming birds sitting on their crowded nests made whole trees look white. Getting closer we began to hear them too: a choir of squeaks, murmurings, croaks and moans interspersed with sharp comments from the jackdaws that also nest in these heronries. Because an often used ride passed close to the colony the birds were quite used to human visitors and sat stolidly on their nests as we watched and noted the carefully organized social structure of the colony. Little and cattle egrets occupied the lower and middle levels of the branches. Above them nested the spoonbills, spread out in a splendid rank all over the rounded tree top, their fine mane-like crests waving in the breeze. And with them the few grey herons ever watchful but not, I think, as wary as ours in Britain. But if any of these flattish or rounded trees had an isolated main stem overtopping the rest, then on this pinnacle was placed the huge nesting platform of a single pair of white storks who seemed to take no heed at all of the noisy multitude below. But they kept a wary eye on every circling kite, either red or black. For kites can change in a flash from birds that float harmlessly aloft into darts that come plunging at anything that looks like food. And that something could be an infant stork.

These woodlands along the *marismas* are the home—almost the last remaining—of one of Europe's noblest and rarest birds, the Spanish imperial eagle. Several were nesting on the Coto Doñana reserve the year we were there and occasionally, chancing to look across the forest, we saw a pair circling above the trees—big, black-looking eagles with bold white bands on their shoulders. Always they were remote and we were content that they should be so. Such rare, shy and wild-spirited eagles are better without man's company and all they need is the preservation of their solitudes. The people of Spain have a marvellous opportunity of earning a conservationist accolade by making a real effort to keep this precious eagle away from what looks dangerously like the road to extinction.

One morning I sat quietly in a glade among the oaks noting the various utterances of the birds: the ceremonial bill-rattling of the storks (if that can be called an utterance) as they changed over duties at the nest; the grunting of spoonbills that seemed to be some sort of alarm-cry; the rasping chatter of great spotted cuckoos as they chased each other wildly through the woods. Occasionally I glimpsed azure-winged magpies, golden orioles and hoopoes in the treetops—all creatures of delight but very fleeting and not nearly as satisfying as the many warblers that were nesting in the bushes all around my clearing. There was a Sardinian warbler with his distinctive black cap, white throat and red eye-ring; a sub-alpine warbler, known by his grey head, pink breast and white moustache; and a rufous warbler, red-backed, white-breasted with a full, reddish, white-ended tail. Up in the trees lived two other warblers more easily heard than seen: the melodious warbler which at treetop height is extremely like a willow warbler and has the same restless way of threading through twigs and delicately picking off insects; and the orphean warbler which looks rather like a blackcap but whose song is thrush-like in the repetition of its phrases. I count it among my most valued memories of Andalusia, this perfect May morning spent with the warblers among the cork oaks.

For these warblers the world, as they find it on the Coto Doñana, is a coloured and fragrant tangle of cistuses, pistachios, halimiums, junipers, tree heaths, brambles and gorse. But it is not an oppressive tangle. It is pierced in all directions by trails of deer and boar. And there are wide spaces adorned by red gladioli, blue irises and a purple-brown orchid called *Serapias lingua*. So flowery and scented a place, lit with such radiant sunlight, seemed a perfect haunt for butterflies: yet there were surprisingly few and they were mostly painted ladies which, lovely as they are, can be met with almost anywhere in Europe, Asia or Africa. Had I come all the way to Andalusia, I wondered, to see only painted ladies? And that was the moment when my first Queen of Spain fritillary chose to alight in a sandy hollow close to where I was sitting. It settled with closed wings that showed off their tawny, silver-spotted undersides—a lovely insect that had at last become a reality instead of a creature I had seen all my life only as a picture in books. But a few minutes later I dropped all thought of butter-flies when, with loud scufflings and gruntings, a female wild boar came bursting out of the yellow-flowered halimium bushes followed by three piglets. A family of wild pigs was something else I had never seen before and what surprised me about them was that though the mother was covered with long black hair, the young were distinctly red and prettily marked with dark horizon-tal bars. Why these habitually nocturnal animals should have been hastening through the scrub in the broad light of day I do not know. All I can say is that as they passed at only five feet distance they never even saw me sitting there with my back against a cork oak. I stayed there some time in the hope (vain as it turned out) that some predator had disturbed this wild boar family and would soon come along on their tracks. A Spanish lynx for instance. For this large, over-persecuted cat, as for the imperial eagle, the Coto Doñana is one of the few remaining refuges. Distinguished from the lynx of north Europe by lines of heavy spots, the Spanish lynx is a beautifully marked animal. But though I looked for it everywhere I never found more than footprints in the sand. We were shown one cooped up in a small pen outside the former hunting lodge that is now the Reserve's headquarters but this merely left me sad and angry, the way I always feel in zoos.

The savanna-like heathland dotted with cork oaks does not end abruptly at the edge of the *marismas*. Between the two zones stretches a broad damp margin of rushy pastures that slope very gently to the estuary. Here we added two further warblers to our list, neither of them easy to observe. One was Savi's warbler which makes a reeling sound in thick cover and would be passed over as a grasshopper warbler if it could sustain its song instead of always stopping and starting. The other warbler was the fan-tailed, at four inches Europe's smallest warbler. It is also Europe's only grass warbler (the genus Cisticola), that numerous group of species so characteristic of Africa, India and south-east Asia and so notorious for causing headaches over their field identification. The fan-tailed warbler, which in Europe is found only in the south, is spread across much of Africa down to the Cape, across Asia to Japan and over the Pacific to the north coast of Australia. It looks rather like a small sedge warbler with a short tail, and since it spends most of its time skulking in deep grass and rushes it is very easily missed. But in the breeding season its song-flight draws attention to it. It mounts high above the ground calling 'zit-zit-zit' (hence its other name of zitting cisticola) as it passes over in jerking flight. But up there against a bright sky this tiny brown warbler can be difficult to see. Most of the time it is just a wandering sound somewhere in the sky. And where fan-tailed warblers are abundant their zitting can be so persistent a background noise that, along with the risping of grasshoppers and the hum of bees, you eventually cease to be aware of it.

Chateaubriand once remarked that forests came before man and that deserts followed him. And at the Coto Doñana you see plenty of evidence that he was right. The arid, semi-desert scrub of the heathland has all the look of secondary vegetation coming in the wake of destroyed forest. Then if you cross this heathland towards the sea you come literally face to face with real desert, a great wall of loose silver sand with 200 square miles of dunes and all the winds of the Atlantic behind it, a wall that advances eastwards

implacably, smothering everything in its path. It is both spectacular and frightening to see this high wave of sand breaking
right over the crowns of not one but whole groves of mature
stone pines. How long, you can't help wondering, before the
whole Guadalquivir estuary and marshlands will disappear under
range after billowing range of dazzling, near-white sand that
already peaks up to form, at 340 feet above sea-level, what well
may be the highest dunes in the whole of Europe?

Not that these dunes are a continuous and uninterrupted stretch
of loose sand. Out in the desert there are pinewoods that somehow manage to survive; and they are the favourite nesting place
of the short-toed eagles that prey on water snakes, Montpellier
snakes, ladder snakes and Lataste's vipers, all of which are said to
be numerous. The pines also attract many small migrant birds that
come down to rest and feed as they might visit an island in the sea.
In the dunes, too, we were told, lived the Thekla lark. This, in
Europe, is a very local bird and the Coto Doñana was the only
place we knew for it. But when we read that the Thekla was
almost indistinguishable in the field from the crested lark I decided
I was not going to fry out there in the dunes looking for so un-
satisfactory a fowl. So I opted for another day on the *marismas*.
But R. S. Thomas wanted his Thekla lark and is a man of deter-
mination. With the sun burning in a cloudless sky I watched his
tall, straight figure get ever smaller as it reached the crest of a far
dune and disappeared into the desert like some Old Testament
prophet who would never again be seen on earth. But that evening
he duly turned up having satisfied himself he had seen his Thekla
lark. I, too, had had my moment. I had seen a small pink cloud of
flamingos moving westward far out over the *marismas*.

Sometime in the fairly recent past the Guadalquivir had a delta
with many mouths. But now blown sand has bottled them all up
except one and practically obliterated the former delta landscape.
The line of one of the lost channels is still to be traced in a string
of attractive pools along the eastward edge of the dunes, pools
that are the haunt of many plants, birds and animals. Here we
glimpsed through bulrushes a purple heron on her nest; we heard
the harsh squawk of the crested coot; saw our first ferruginous

ducks and red-crested pochards; but failed to see white-headed duck, marbled duck or purple gallinule, all three of which you need a slice of luck to find there.

From the Coto Doñana, when the air was clear, we looked inland across the *marismas* to the alluring Sierra de Ronda whose rugged summits rise against the eastern sky to nearly seven thousand feet. So because the coastal region was so hot and the mountains looked so cool; and because our bird-lists were most in need of mountain species, it was to the uplands we decided to go when we left Doñana.

The Ronda mountains cover nearly a thousand square miles of harsh and broken country, much of it arid limestone, a thinly populated region with far-scattered villages and one or two spectacular, high-level towns. Of the villages I especially remember Grazalema, so attractive with its terracotta roofs, white-washed walls and narrow streets. From its remote mountain shelf Grazalema looks to wild and distant sierras and is itself dominated by a pallid thousand-foot crag of creviced limestone, a crag noted for its especially beautiful narcissi: but you have to be there in April to see them. If you are a connoisseur of country towns you will travel far in Europe before you find one more striking than Ronda, an ancient place set well over two thousand feet above the sea and cleft in two by a three-hundred-foot deep gorge spanned by a massive eighteenth-century bridge that is a triumph of engineering. On this bridge you can be happy a long time watching choughs, swifts and lesser kestrels playing in the wind. You may see a peregrine, a vulture or some exciting eagle wheeling round; or merely the rock-sparrows nesting in cracks in the masonry. And if there are no birds at all it is still a wonderful place, this great chasm in the crumbling sandstone, with the old town above and the torrent called Guadalevin a thread of silver far down in the shadows.

Till recent years there have been few good roads through these mountains and many awful ones; but tourism is changing all that. Good or bad, these roads lead you across delightfully rocky and open country that is still quite flowery. But for how much longer? For the ever-nibbling goats that have no equal as destroyers of vegetation, roam everywhere in large herds. No doubt they have played a key part in reducing the once far-spreading cork-oak forests of these uplands to the small relict patches you find up there today. The same with the Spanish fir (*Abies pinsapo*) whose world distribution as a native is restricted to north-facing lime-stone slopes of these Ronda mountains. Very distinctive because of its short stiff needles, this rare conifer, though such a lime-lover on its native soil, grows well when planted even on acid soils in Britain, as you can see in the National Trust garden at Bodnant in north Wales where one was planted in 1876 and now makes a tree about a hundred feet tall.

Camping in these mountains was pure delight after the Coto Doñana. For up here the nights were cool and entirely without mosquitoes. We dropped into sleep listening to nightingales, red-necked nightjars, common nightjars (and the inescapable goat-bells) and we woke at dawn to the harsh shouts of great grey shrikes, the gentle cooing of turtle doves and the songs of melodious warblers (which to me are not remarkably melodious, achieving something between the rich song of a garden warbler and the scratchy tune of a whitethroat). One of our camps was near an escarpment where the limestone had weathered and shat-tered to form a precipice full of caverns and deep fissures. And here many vultures were nesting. We scrambled from the road to the foot of this great crag up steep slopes rough with block scree and oak bushes and for once were grateful to the goats. For the oak there was the Kermes oak which, though reaching only a few feet in height, was quite as prickly as holly and made a jungle that would have been quite impenetrable if goats had not criss-crossed it in all directions by their trails.

Two kinds of vulture were breeding on these cliffs: griffons mainly and a few Egyptians. The huge griffons perched promi-nently along the rocky skyline, managing to look aloof and in-different yet never, I think, really taking their eyes off us. Occasion-ally they sailed out to circle slowly over us with rarely a flap of their vast square wings. But when a goat-herd came following his flock across the scree a griffon swooshed down with a thunderous *woomp* of wings a few yards above the man's head. Then the bird went straight back to its crag to resume its silent, unemotional pose. The Egyptian vultures were even less demonstrative: but were more beautiful to see gliding along the pale rock face, their black and white plumage gleaming in the sun's bright light. To me their outline against the sky and the stiff way they held their wings suggested some huge and strange sort of fulmar. We had a final moment of excitement as a new bird came sailing along the cliff top, a large raptor which, from below, had a white head and body contrasting with long dark wings. Then it banked to show a clear white bar down the centre of its back. It was our first Bonelli's eagle. A species of the southern fringe of Europe, and much better known in Africa and India, this beautiful eagle is one of the many birds of prey that are in urgent need of protection in Europe.

Below the vulture crag we came upon a splendid lizard. For anyone who knows only the darting little brown lizards of Britain it is one of the most delightful shocks of natural history suddenly to be confronted with a lizard that is well over two feet long, brilliantly green and generously spotted with bright yellow and blue. You really do feel you're getting near the tropics. But it did not wait to be admired, this gorgeous ocellated lizard. A quick scuttling movement, a rasping of claws against bark and it was away up a tree trunk and gone.

Then, soon after, a snake crossed our path, much to R. S. Thomas's delight. He is, I would say, a particularly snake-conscious man. Before going to Spain he evidently did some herpetological homework because he had several times relieved the tedium of motoring across Spain by giving me lectures on the snakes we might encounter in Andalusia. He spoke often of the terrors of Lataste's viper and I think he was disappointed we had met so few. Even on the Coto Doñana we had seen hardly the tail of one disappearing into cover. But now at last here was a most satisfactory serpent nearly four feet long right at our feet and giving us a leisurely view of itself as it slowly moved off. It was slender and medium-brown with two thin dark lines going parallel down the length of its back. Joining them at regular intervals were many short cross-bars: hence this species' name, the ladder snake. Like all European snakes, the vipers excepted, the ladder snake is non venomous.

To us who know the chough as a precarious species clinging to the mild fringes of western Britain and Ireland, it was a revelation to see how abundant the bird is in these warm southern mountains. We found nesting pairs in many places and near El Burgo saw a large flock of presumably non-breeders rising and plunging as if in a ballet dance in the breezes funnelling through a gorge. Here spotless starlings chorused cheerfully about their nest-holes in the cliffs (till then we had seen them only on houses and trees); and male rock-buntings, cleanly stroked with black lines across their silver-grey cheeks, perched stolidly on boulders and repeated toneless notes with true bunting persistence. Another new bird for us was the black wheatear, a really aristocratic-looking member of its family because of its superior size and the eye-catching splash of white on rump and tail that contrasts so perfectly with the solid blackness of the rest of the plumage. Red-rumped swallow and alpine swift completed our mountain tally. About our identification of the pallid swift we continued to feel uneasy: we saw many 'possible probables' without ever being able to swear that they were not common swifts.

Goats had not eaten all the wildflowers. A shrubby grey sage with purple-pink flowers (*Phlomis purpurea*) was an adornment of many a slope; and occasionally a whole hillside was gay with cistus flowers, some all-white, some white with chocolate centres, some purple-red. Man orchids and late spider orchids were frequent and one wet place was solidly purple-red over many square yards with the tall and elegant loose-flowered orchid (*Orchis laxiflora*). Dry stream-beds were pink with oleanders. Tall, white-flowered asphodels and equally attractive stars-of-Bethlehem graced the roadsides. Viper's bugloss spread lavish purple-blue patches on banks. A cream and pink figwort called *Bellardia trixago* stays in my memory as an especial joy. So does the remarkable *Scilla peruviana* which has a rounded mass of violet-blue flowers rising from wide, green, strap-like basal leaves. Two bindweeds were colourful: *Convolvulus tricolor*, delicately pale blue, white and yellow; and *C. altheoides* which is a bright purple-pink.

Most spectacular was the giant fennel whose great yellow umbels towered over our heads. Most curious was the dwarf fan palm, Europe's only native palm but which is a mere fountain of leaves at ground level, lacking any trunk to bear them aloft. Most alarming was the sight of the alien prickly pear escaping into the wild in rocky places along the mountain roads. We thought with dread of its rapid and devastating colonization of thousands of square miles of eastern Australia's sheep pastures and wondered if the delectable Sierra de Ronda were doomed to a similar fate.

With regret we left these fair mountains for the long drive north. But one last Andalusian splendour was promised—a roadside lake where we had been told we might see flamingoes, a lake which, when we first sighted it across the plain, seemed a thoroughly domesticated sheet of water. For it was overlooked by a sizeable village and there were fields of barley and sunflowers all round, olive groves farther back and men shouting to their mules as they tilled the nearby crops. Not a place for flamingoes, we reckoned. We had always thought of them as belonging to the greater wildernesses of the world, not to roadside lakes with herds of goats in the foreground. But it doesn't do to romanticize too much about birds and wild places. It's not only sparrows and starlings that will accept man on intimate terms. A dotterel may delight in a pool outside a steel-works. A peregrine may nest on a skyscraper. Wagtails will roost on a city railway station. And a warm salt-lake rich in plankton will be found by flamingoes no matter how tamed its surroundings.

So, when we looked through our binoculars at this unpromising pool, there, prominent in the foreground, were our flamingoes, three hundred of them wading in a shallow bay at the nearest end of the lake. Large and mainly white, with an S-shaped neck occasionally visible, they were at that range very swan-like. They did not become real picture-book flamingoes till we were much nearer and could see the patch of bright crimson each carried on its wing and the strange shape of their beaks when heads were lifted. But most of the time they kept their long, thin necks vertically downwards and their heads under water as they sifted the mud: so that they looked like a close-packed crowd of headless round white bodies each supported by three long legs. That night we camped at the lake edge with the flamingos near by. Until then we had not realized how noisy they are. We fell asleep to their goose-like honking, heard it several times during the night and woke to it again at dawn.

The lake had many other birds. Migrant spotted redshanks, greenshanks, ruffs, knots, sanderlings, dunlins and wood sandpipers foraged round the drying margins with dozens of stilts and avocets. Along shingle bars extending into the lake scores of Kentish plovers were obviously breeding. Pratincoles swooped low over the water taking flies with the utmost grace. High above them circled a pair of gull-billed terns. Coot, mallard and pochard were everywhere. There were a few gadwall and, at last, the marbled duck we had failed to find on the Coto Doñana. Great reed-warblers sang in the rushes; fan-tailed warblers lisped unseen in the air; quail called their three quick notes in the fields; calandra larks sang loud and clear all around us; crested and short-toed larks rose into flight as we walked round the water's edge.

Given a whole year at this lake an observer would, I think, record a wonderful selection of Europe's birds. It is one of those rare and special places whither birds seem called from the four ends of the earth. Long may it remain thus unpolluted and unexploited. In north Europe a water so abounding with life would be a well-wardened bird sanctuary. In south Spain who knows what may happen? You have only to see the devastating effect of the holiday industry on the coast to realize how precarious could be the future of inland waters also. So I pray that inspired by success on the Coto Doñana, the conservationist movement in Spain will go on gathering strength and be able to safeguard many of the other places known to be rich in animals, birds and plants whose future is threatened by developments of every description. Andalusia alone has very many choice areas that would make superb nature reserves. Indeed the whole province should be given special status as a conservation area before it is totally ruined by tourism, rice fields and a hundred other undesirable changes.

᏶ᴥᏜ 7. A High Park in Africa

Some time ago the American naturalist Edwin Way Teale wrote a book he called *North with the Spring* in which he described how, travelling up through the United States and then Canada, he kept pace with greening leaf and flying bird as the tide of the seasons swept up from the tropics to the arctic. A happy idea that made a charming book. And some day perhaps someone will oblige us with 'South with the Autumn'. It is certainly a book I would like to write myself. It would be a book full of migrant birds and about following them down their long southward safari. The millions of warblers, flycatchers, redstarts, whinchats, wheatears, tree pipits, shrikes, nightingales, nightjars, swifts, swallows, martins, ducks and waders which, having summered in the northlands, retreat southwards in September and October—somehow I would go with them on their road back to the heart of Africa.

Back to Africa. Back to the vast salty lakes, to the unlimited plains and acacia savannas, to the shades of the great Congo forests, to papyrus-thickets choking swamps the size of Scotland, to the miombo woodlands that go on for nearly two thousand miles. In uncountable numbers the birds are absorbed into the great continent and of their lives there comparatively little is yet known. The same with many of Africa's resident birds: their habits have not been studied, their movements are untraced. Even the nests and eggs of some have yet to be described. Inevitably bird-students from other continents feel strongly the lure of Africa. Some go with package tours on the round of well-known parks. Others go as single spies or small groups venturing to unmapped wildernesses. There can be few who are not deeply moved by all they see.

To Africa: it is a journey I dreamed of making ever since in my youth I first learned of these great migrations, these tidal surges of birds from tropics to temperate zone and back again. For these were always my favourite birds, the far travellers that appeared each spring so mysteriously to enrich woods and hedgerows, marshes and lakesides with their songs and courtships. And were gone at the summer's end.

Then one day I was able to fulfil this desire. It was when Penny and I were invited to go and stay with our Welsh botanist friend, Mary Richards, who was studying the flora of central Africa and who had taken a house at Mbala, a high-placed little town above the southern end of Lake Tanganyika. 'It's wonderful out here,' she wrote. (All her letters glowed with excitement.) 'There are birds absolutely everywhere. Why don't you come and write a book about them all? You can stay with me as long as you like.' So to Zambia we went. And from there we ventured over the border into one of the wildest parts of Tanzania. Our five months exploring that part of the western arm of the Great Rift Valley with Mary Richards I described in my book *Birds and Wild Africa*.

That trip took place a dozen years ago when Mary Richards was already no longer young. Since then she has kept at her plant-seeking with unfailing enthusiasm and has only just retired at the age of eighty-nine. For more than twenty years she has ventured into the harshest regions of east Africa's plains and mountains, some of which even today are scarcely known to anyone. How many women have been more fascinated by the outdoor life, have spent more nights under canvas in the wild places than she has? If only we all had a dream and a goal as strong and as innocent as Mary Richards's passion for field botany. . . .

On our first visit to Africa Penny and I also experienced true wilderness: we saw lakes, rivers, valleys, swamps, plains, savannas and forests all blessed with a superabundance of wildlife, and all outside national parks. But in books and magazines there was so much talk of the wonders (and problems) of Tsavo, Serengeti, Ngorongoro and other parks and reserves that I felt curious to visit some of them to see how they worked. This I have since been able to do. All the parks I have seen (though one can criticize details here and there) are magnificently successful and an inspiration to conservationists the world over. And a park that especially appeals to me for its variety and scenic splendour (but is not among the most celebrated) is the National Park of Arusha in northern Tanzania close to the Kenya border.

Though this beautiful park is only a few miles off the main route between Tsavo and Ngorongoro, most people miss it simply because they are lured on by those more famous names. Or they miss it because they are on a safari organized by tour-operators who have convinced themselves that the only animals people want to see are lions and still more lions (of which there is not a trace in Arusha Park). So their clients speed along the tarmac of the main road and when, near Arusha, they see a great lone peak building up close in the north, their guide tells them its name is Meru but, probably because he has never been to it, he neglects to say that up there on Meru's slopes is one of the most attractive parks in all Africa.

And so unique. None of the sun-scorched, far-spreading, acacia-scattered plains you find in most other parks. Hardly any flatness anywhere. Instead the landscape is totally restless, a land that speaks everywhere of turmoil and pain not far within the crust of the earth. So this Park of Arusha (the town is only twenty miles away) is emphatically a three-dimensional place. From its lowest levels, at 5,000 feet above the sea, you look westward up and up the face of evergreen forests that reach to near 9,000 feet and are topped by cliffs that climb sheer for another few thousand. Above them the slopes go on and up through an alpine zone to the snow-touched summit of Mount Meru which, at nearly 15,000 feet, is the fifth highest mountain in Africa. Then you turn to the east and look across what in Africa is a most unusual landscape: a world of volcanic hills and ridges separated by little lakes with interesting, irregular slopes. And beyond, thirty miles away, Kilimanjaro, Africa's highest mountain, loses its snowy dome far up in the haze. Meru and Kilimanjaro are sister mountains, twin ex-volcanoes that sit side by side on an island above the surrounding plains. And like many an island in the ocean this lofty, isolated volcanic plateau has its animals and plants that are found nowhere else in the world.

Kilimanjaro as a volcano is long, long extinct. But Meru erupted only a century ago and so can show you many of the features of a recent volcano—fresh-looking craters, lava flows, ash cones and the mudflows of volcanic material that geologists call lahars. Meru is just one of a string of volcanoes that bulged up out of the plain about the end of the Cretaceous period and, with the simultaneous splitting open of the Great Rift Valley, changed the face of east Africa.

Meru's career has been sensational. Time after time it must have erupted, piling itself up until its cone may once have looked down on Kilimanjaro itself. Then came disaster. Perhaps some massive snow-cap or a crater lake dropped into the volcano's vent during an eruption, causing a phenomenal pressure of steam. A super-explosion blew thousands of feet off the summit, especially on the east, leaving Meru the broken and hollowed mountain it is today. Everywhere in the Park and beyond, you see the results of the cataclysm: especially the vast avalanche of rock, rubble, ash and mud that went sliding towards Kilimanjaro, flowing across the country for fifteen miles, blocking the original drainage and creating a new pattern of lakes and streams among hills of volcanic debris.

So Meru lost its summit in an ancient calamity. But eruptions on a vast scale continued and from the floor of the great cavity (or caldera) left behind by the explosion (it is several miles across) a new pyramid of ash began to build up. And this still stands, a volcano within a volcano, a splendid sharp cone that peaks up to 3,000 feet from the floor of the old caldera. Even at that height its summit is easily overlooked by the cliffs that surround it on three sides. It is a real scenic spectacle as well as being a marvellous geological specimen, this tall and perfect cone standing in the middle of the ancient caldera.

A motorable track (for strong vehicles only) has been made up the slopes of Meru as far as the caldera. Here, where the evergreen forest ends and the zone of the tree heath begins, you can walk through wide grassy glades that lead on round the caldera rim. Near vast and ancient trees along the forest's higher edge a log cabin has been perfectly sited to look up to the shapely ash cone and the great cliffs across the crater. You also look down into a ravine that a river off the upper heights has sliced into the

H

caldera floor. It is a wilderness of great peace and beauty: yet at the same time full of tumultuous, disturbing ideas about the tensions and instability of the earth. Occasionally a distant rumble breaks the silence and you look up to see a plume of dust where rocks, loosened by the alternation of all-year-round nightly frost and midday heat, have cracked from ever-crumbling precipices. You get the feeling of a youthful landscape being shaped by vigorous forces as you watch. And you may not always feel sure that some of those plumes of dust are not in fact puffs of vapour escaping from fumaroles. There is, you recall, a volcano not far away, Ol Doinyo Ngai (The Mountain of God), that is still fairly active. So you would scarcely be surprised if Meru, too, erupted here and now.

Sooner or later you turn back into the forest that extends down from the caldera for 2,000 feet. It is a double-tier evergreen forest dominated by two magnificent species of conifer: the African pencil-cedar which is in fact a juniper (*Juniperus procera*) and the east African yellow-wood (*Podocarpus gracilior*) usually known simply as podo. In few places anywhere in Africa today will you find a better example of this type of montane forest: for these great conifers have been long and terribly exploited nearly everywhere and survive here on Meru only because of their remoteness. Though subjected to an annual dry season it is a forest with some of the qualities of true equatorial rain-forest. The over-canopy of cedar and podo must be at least 120 feet above ground. The under-canopy is of broad-leaved trees—ilex, afrocrania, nuxia, olive—some of which are near the size of English oaks. Branches stream with beards of moss and lichen, or bristle with ferns and orchids. Lianas hang everywhere. Here and there great trees have been smothered by the aerial roots of strangler figs. There is deep shade and coolness everywhere except in the glades that form where a giant tree has crashed and let in gales that have then brought down its neighbours.

It is not an impenetrable type of forest, most of it. But you need to watch out for stinging nettles of which there seems to be a species for attacking every altitude of your body, not to mention those overhead nettles that are the size of trees and have hard woody trunks. Away from the nettle beds you can often walk as easily through the trees as through a Chiltern beechwood. And if you do find yourself faced by thickets you are usually helped through them by animal trails, for even in these mountain forests there are many buffaloes and elephants. Not that much is ever seen of them because they spend the day hidden in the recesses of the forest though they evidently move about a great deal at night.

It is different with the colobus monkeys: they go round in gangs and don't mind at all showing themselves as they advance gaily through the treetops, crashing from one bough to another and shouting all the time to warn other troops to keep clear. Magnificently pelaged in black and white (the white part hangs like a loosely worn cape) the colobus always looks dressed up for a ceremony. Inevitably, in unprotected areas, such an attractive animal is frequently hunted and you quite often see Africans draped in colobus pelts; and by long tradition the Chagga people of Kilimanjaro use colobus fur in their tribal head-dresses. But these are minor predations that offer no threat to colobus numbers. What is a real menace, however, is that colobus rugs have become a popular item in the east African tourist trade, especially in Kenya, and thousands of what are perhaps the world's most beautiful monkeys are being slaughtered. This trafficking should be made illegal everywhere, before the colobus goes the way of the crocodile which, so common till fairly recently, has now become scarce: and all because of the ruthless and conscienceless skin trade.

Birds in the Meru forest are abundant. This much your ears soon tell you. But as always in leafy trees, to get a view of the birds you need patience and it is best to be out by dawn. You find a clearing and a log to sit on (taking care to avoid the siafu— the terrible safari ants that are the scourge of the forest). Then you wait and watch until perhaps your neck begins to ache with so much upward craning. There will be long periods when you see nothing and all you can do is to listen in frustration to unknown songs and cries. But you may at last get glimpses, however brief, of warblers, greenbuls, flycatchers, honey-guides, cuckoo-shrikes, bush-shrikes, twin-spots and others. How many you will name correctly from such fleeting views I will not prophesy, for some can be difficult. So why not let technology help you? The modern way of observing forest birds is to tape-record their calls and play them back on the spot both loud and clear. The effect can be dramatic. Anxious to find out what rivals are daring to invade, even the most secretive little birds will come venturing out of cover and display themselves as if summoned by Orpheus and his lute.

The forest's chief noise-producers (apart from colobus monkeys) include silvery-cheeked hornbills, red-headed parrots, francolins (at dawn and dusk) and Hartlaub's turacos. Between them they treat the world to an unending chorus of squeaks, squawks, quacks, barks, growls, braying, crowing, shrieking and cackling—all great-voiced sounds that carry far through the trees. Among other large birds is the mountain buzzard that wheels overhead like the common buzzard of Europe and looks and sounds almost exactly the same. There is also the African goshawk, always an exciting bird to come upon and which is perhaps not uncommon but, as with all such shy hawks, you are lucky if you see one. Most majestic of all, king of the forest if you like, is the crowned hawk-eagle, a massive, heavily barred raptor you may find lurking near a troop of colobus monkeys, for they are its commonest prey. And perhaps, happening to look up from some clearing, you might see the long-winged shape of a bearded vulture crossing the sky towards the caldera cliffs where they are thought to breed.

Of the small birds I saw in the forest a few are still vivid in my memory. The strange-looking, broad-ringed white-eye that is like a bright yellow warbler but is remarkable for the very conspicuous white band round its eye. The Tacazze sunbirds (the males are purple-black with long slender tails) taking nectar from flowers only four feet from my upturned face. A redstart-like bird called the white-starred bush-robin that now and then dashed across the track showing a slate-blue back and an arresting golden rump. A couple of companion species, the rough-wing swallow that is all black and the cinnamon-chested bee-eater which is full of colour: they nested close to each other in holes in trackside banks. Two of Africa's most local starlings, best known in the forests of Meru and Kilimanjaro: Kenrick's starling which is black and Abbot's starling, black above and white below—they were feeding in a mixed flock on the fruits of a climber that hung like a curtain high in a tree. Near them, perhaps significantly so, an African hobby perched motionless, its deep chestnut breast distinguishing it from the European hobby.

Where in east Africa are doves not among the most numerous and most vocal of all birds? So in the forest on Meru there is the pink-breasted dove, the bronze-naped pigeon and the olive pigeon. All fruitarians—doves, starlings, turacos, hornbills—lead a wandering life, pausing a few days here and there where they find fruit in season. Wild figs are especially important in their lives. So are wild olives and juniper berries. But having said that you have said practically all that is known about some of the birds that live in the depths of the forest. Or should I say the heights? For several are treetop species whose life-histories will be the very last to be unravelled. One little bird I saw in the mountain forest was the Abyssinian hill-babbler. A soft grey-brown all over—or so it appeared in the dim green light among the trees—it looked to me rather like a hedge-sparrow. But its song must be something special. 'Fine, clear and nightingale-like,' says one observer. 'The finest songster in Africa,' says another. For me it uttered not a whisper of a note. But isn't this a good enough reason for going back to that perfect forest some day at the right season?

Butterflies of many sizes and colours swoop about you through the forest. There is the long-tailed admiral, an obvious cousin of the red admiral of Europe and whose caterpillars, like the red admiral's, feed on nettles. But most butterflies I saw were various charaxes and papilios. The trouble with the gorgeous charaxes is that they tend to fly very high and if you want to interview them you have to lure them down with ripe bananas, rotten meat or even dung. So it is the papilios flashing by at eye-level that give most joy. The swallowtail (*Papilio phorcas*) is one of the commonest and is remarkable because, although almost entirely black with merely a stripe of green across the wing, it can appear, because of the effects of scintillation, as a total dazzle of green. Also abundant is the Meru race of the Kilimanjaro swallowtail. But how local: these forests of Mount Meru between seven and nine thousand feet are its total world range. So by long segregation the highest peaks of Africa have all evolved their unique forms of life.

The face of the forest is scored by gorges loud with waterfalls and so tangled by thorny bushes, wild date-palms and thick-stemmed lianas as to be impenetrable without the many elephant trails. If up till now you have thought of the elephant as an animal that is happy only on fairly level ground, here you see him in a new light as a scrambler down difficult ravines, a squeezer through narrow gullies, a scaler of slippery rocks. What brings him exploring these narrow defiles is the need for water. The dry season is long and elephants must drink and bathe the whole year round. So everywhere you find evidence of their adventurings: their well-worn paths, their frequent droppings, the tree bark polished smooth where their bodies have pushed by. But though these trails are so useful to man they have one serious hazard: they can be awkward places in which to meet with elephants face to face. You need to keep your eye well ahead so that you see them coming. (Far better to take a game-scout to do this for you.) Then by the time the elephants arrive you have drawn discreetly aside. Do that and they pass quite happily, for elephants normally wish peace upon the world.

When I found myself in the heart of these high Meru forests my first impression was of the strangeness of everything about me: the great boles of the cedars and the podos, the many unknown trees and shrubs, the branches bearded with new ferns, lichens and orchids, the clearings glowing with fire-ball lilies, red-hot pokers and bright red indigoferas. Yet to my surprise after a little while I began to find old friends among the plants. On a cool and shady bank I found a patch of wood sanicle, then a carpet of wood sorrel, a few plantains, lady's mantles, even violets. Not quite the same species as we know in Britain, but very close to them. And in the ravines there were filmy ferns, soft shieldferns, green spleen-worts and hartstongue ferns that would have looked perfectly at home in many a wet gully in Wales. So just as the alpine flora of

Switzerland has much in common with that of the arctic, so some of the high-altitude plants of Africa are little different from those of temperate Europe.

As you come down through Meru's forests you gradually leave behind the great pencil cedars and podos for they belong to the cooler heights frequently soaked by mountain mist. Below 7,000 feet you are in forest mainly of olives of three kinds, their distribution dictated by their differing water needs. The species are loliondo (*Olea welwitschii*), brown olive (*O. africana*) and east African olive (*O. hochstetteri*). It is a type of forest that until the beginning of this century covered all the lower levels of what is now the National Park. Since 1900 much of this easily accessible lower forest has been cleared, for olive is a valuable multipurpose timber used in various parts of east Africa for furniture, floor blocks, railway fuel and all sorts of buildings. Some of the cleared forest became farming land and so, outside the Park, it still is. Within the Park the forest has been replaced by sage scrub and tussocky grassland.

There are then two halves to this Park, an upper and a lower. The upper is a natural zone, partly bare mountain, partly primal forest. The lower, its forests now destroyed, is being invaded by replacement vegetation which, being extremely wayward and wilful, brings with it severe problems of management. The question is: in the interests of conservation which way will it be best for the vegetation to develop? Should it be encouraged to go back to forest? This at first glance might seem the most sensible goal. For true forest, in east Africa, is something rather rare. But an opposite point of view is that in a Park already half under forest, the last thing needed is still more forest. Better—so the argument goes—better to go in for more diversity of habitat and develop some open ground for antelopes and other animals of the plains. A forest's wildlife may be immensely rich but to observe it you need infinite leisure and patience. Forests have therefore relatively little to offer to the average out-of-breath safari tourists whose entrance money is the mainstay of the Park, for they are driven on by the remorseless time-tables of the tour operators.

There is a further, much graver difficulty about trying to restore the forest—the lack of suitable soil. For the ancient forest soils have now been lost. Exposed by the axe to fierce sun and drought throughout the dry season, then pounded by tropical rain with its headlong run-off, these soils, the product of unknown centuries of delicate chemistry on the forest floor, were quickly blown or scoured away. Man—ecological, conservationist man—can come on the scene later and utter fine phrases about recycling the processes of nature back to a state of productivity, but he won't do it in five minutes. The raped soil's lost virtue will be restored only very gradually through long and complicated successions of vegetation. Perhaps, for instance, the sage scrub could be guided into becoming acacia woodland in the hope (for it is only a hope) that after the acacias might come a regeneration of evergreen forest as the humus improves in quality.

So we come back to the alternative of accepting that this area now covered by secondary scrub will never again grow forest but might be converted to profitable grassland which in national park terms means pasture rich enough to support a numerous population of game animals. Once established, such grassland should be self-perpetuating because the grazing mammals keep it cut and prevent it from turning into scrub. But the creation of these permanent pastures can meet with difficulties. In Arusha Park, for instance, there is drought to be faced and there are mole-rats. The answer to drought is irrigation from the perennial streams off Meru. But mole-rats are a different problem. These multitudinous, red-brown, furry rodents, about eight inches long, burrow everywhere through the soil, constantly loosening it and preventing grasses from getting a root-hold. When I visited that part of the Park a heavy roller was being used to flatten the mole-rat runs and to consolidate the ground. But then maybe next day along would come a herd of elephants who thought this beautifully rolled terrain made a perfect dust bathing area, for the earth was like a fine volcanic ash. By the time they had finished with it the field had turned into a patch of rough desert on which the wind got to work, and soon all that was left was a mosaic of dust bowls.

The man who told me about these delicate management decisions and experiments was the late Desmond Vesey-FitzGerald whom I had met before in Zambia when he was chief scientific officer at the International Red Locust Control headquarters at Mbala. Now, having reached retirement, he had launched zestfully into a new career in the Tanzania National Park service. But no one who knew him was surprised. He was one of the most enthusiastic all-round nature conservationists in Africa and an expert on subjects as diverse as grasshoppers, dragonflies, birds, frogs, snakes and mammals. His work on locusts gave him a deep insight into the ecology of grasslands and this knowledge he had now turned to a different purpose—the management of savannas for antelopes, buffaloes, zebras, giraffes and their fellow grazers and browsers.

Vesey (so everyone called him) was a believer in the animals themselves as the keepers of their own habitats. Especially if given a little guidance. Carefully manipulated they could be a most effective tool of management. His especial love was the elephant. Though there are plenty of elephants in Arusha Park and though they grievously maltreat the beautiful yellow-barked acacias, he accepted this as part of the natural order and would have little to do with wholesale elephant destruction such as goes on in some national parks. Where this culling had taken place he asked the question: are the results being carefully monitored so that in future we shall know for sure whether such killing is justified? He himself doubted if they were. Too often man is eager to intervene violently in nature. Too rarely is he prepared to go to the sweat of undertaking the long and patient research that should precede and follow each act of intervention. For most people, and especially the active, out-door type of man attracted to work in national parks and nature reserves, it is so much easier to act than to think. But just because we see lovely groves of acacias being devastated by elephants we have no right to conclude that this is something new in the world. It may always have been an important part of African ecology. Nature has her own methods of dealing with population explosions. And in east Africa she can control elephant numbers by drought as happened not long ago in Tsavo National Park. I am sure that what African wildlife conservation needs is more and more thoughtful ecologists like

Vesey-FitzGerald and fewer of the hairy-chested, men-of-action type of game wardens who can do so much damage by over-hasty, ill-conceived decisions.

Most visitors to Arusha National Park do not venture far up Mount Meru where the forest roads are rough and wildlife so elusive. Instead people prefer to drive round the lower, more open sections of the Park, following roads that thread easily along the edges of the Momela Lakes, so attractively set among the volcanic ridges. In this land of low-profile hills separated by irregularly shaped waters there are herds of buffaloes and elephants and plenty of giraffes, waterbucks, bushbucks, reedbucks, wart-hogs, baboons and vervet monkeys—all easy to see in the thin bush and grasslands that cover the whole scene. There are also a few black rhinos: usually they are alone, grazing placidly or merely standing and looking at the world as if chewing over rhino thoughts that have not altered since the Pleistocene Age. One lake only, Small Momela, has hippos. As for the absence of lions, I found it refreshing to be in a park where there is none of that incessant and fatuous pursuing of lions by cars which so detracts from the wilderness atmosphere of places like Serengeti and Ngorongoro. Incidentally, it was also good to be in a park that has neither mosquitoes nor tsetse flies.

Lakeside birds are plentiful—egrets, herons, ibises, spoonbills, pelicans, flamingoes, ducks, geese, waders and lily trotters—for these food-rich waters range from fresh to highly alkaline. At one pool a bird arrived that I had looked for in vain in Europe. This was a black stork which came spiralling down from the sky as unannounced as a meteorite. He stood quite still for half an hour in shallow water, tall, elegant, white-breasted, his dark back glossed purple and green. Then, rested, he took off again as suddenly as he had arrived. He rose circling above the trees until, finding the upper breezes, he was soon beyond sight.

On one of these lakes—it is called Tulusia—I first saw flamingoes swimming. All of a hot afternoon they had stood in a sleepily preening group ankle-deep in water. But as the day's light began to fade they trooped into the lake until out of their depth, then swam purposefully a few hundred yards out (where it may be a hundred feet deep) and began feeding by swishing their heavy-looking bills from side to side just under the surface. Have they developed this habit because an ambrosial store of algae (truly the food of the gods to flamingoes) rises to the surface at night? Certainly these alkaline lakes are extremely algiferous; so much so that they are liable to suffer from those acute population explosions called algal blooms. Big Momela Lake, when I saw it, was an unhealthy whitish-yellow, thick, soupy, poisonous and stinking from half-a-mile away of rotten eggs. And, of course, no birds. Yet six months later I heard that it had cleared itself and was again quite wholesome and attractive to the many maccoa ducks and others that can live in very alkaline waters.

Birds of light bush country are abundant round the lakes. I recall spotted-flanked barbets, black cuckoo-shrikes, yellow bishops, red-collared widowbirds and two palearctic migrants, the red-backed and red-tailed shrikes. There was also the red-throated tit, a bird quite remarkably like a female chaffinch. It is a species that occupies but a little space in the world, being found only in south Kenya and northern Tanzania. Another rather local bird, but very striking, was the brown-breasted barbet that has a vividly scarlet head and throat, brown mantle, wings and breast, and a white rump and belly.

When a buffalo died near the lakes I kept a close eye on it, expecting hourly that vultures would come crowding to it for they frequently passed high overhead on their endless reconnaissances. In the event no vulture came near this buffalo for nearly a week and then not until hyenas came one night and ripped the carcass open. Next morning it was covered by a mound of quarrelling, flapping, hissing and swearing white-backed vultures. They looked a formidable crowd with their great beaks threatening all comers. Yet three white-headed vultures who arrived simply charged into the middle of the scrum without hesitation or harm. So, later on, did a Ruppell's griffon, a handsome vulture covered all over the brown wings with big white spots. Then came five marabou storks. They landed a few feet away and elbowed their way hugely and contemptuously among the bickering vultures, helping themselves as they pleased. Last to arrive was a lappet-faced vulture. I was particularly interested to see how he would acquit himself for he has the reputation of being king of the vultures and first in the pecking order. For his reputation's sake let us say that this one wasn't very hungry: for he stood aloof and alone, waiting his turn along with the smaller hooded vultures, ten of which stood round in a timid circle, hoping for scraps.

A very special area of Arusha Park is Ngurdoto Crater, site of a volcano, long ago extinct, that stood a dozen miles south-east of Mount Meru. Before the great explosion that blew off Meru's summit, the pent-up forces beneath had been breaking out as parasitic cones, one of the largest of which was Ngurdoto. This, like Meru itself, has long ago collapsed to form a caldera. But unlike Meru's caldera, which is shattered on one side, Ngurdoto's is still perfect all round, a flat-bottomed, circular cavity two miles across and looked down on all round by a tree-covered escarpment. To see into it you follow a motorable track up through the forest to viewpoints on the caldera rim. From there you look down on to a partly swamp-covered, partly tree-scattered plain as if you were a spectator in an amphitheatre. Several hundred feet below you mixed herds of buffaloes, elephants, rhinos, antelopes and wart-hogs graze and browse in perfect freedom from human interference: for this is the one section of the Park that no one is allowed to enter, not even members of the Park staff except under special circumstances. It is a reserve within a reserve; what a crime it would be to admit people into this paradise. Let them gaze into it from above but never enter.

If, out of all the game reserves and parks I have visited, I had to suggest one locality that I feel most authentically retains the spirit and atmosphere of truly wild Africa I would choose this untouched little crater of Ngurdoto that is guarded so beautifully by its cliffs and mantling forests. Here a man could come, maybe some drooping conservationist in need of refreshment of mind; and he could look down on this Arcadia for long tranquil hours or even days. There he could sit and think with the great forest trees about him, listening to unseen birds, observing the peaceful animals below and watching the vultures and eagles that from time to time swing lazily out of the crags to circle slowly over the crater. He could not fail to be strengthened by the thought that despite the destructive changes going on throughout the world there are still some wonderful places that man has had the wisdom to set aside to be handed on to the future with their fauna, flora and all their beauty intact: specimens of the natural world, the old world, our planet as it was before man laid his hands too greedily upon it. He would see, I trust, that if such a masterpiece of conservation can be achieved in one place, others could be achieved elsewhere. And he would go on his way with a new heart for the struggle.

8. Wilderness Scotland

It was two books, a statistic and an invitation that took us to north Scotland. The invitation came from our old friends Cecil and Jonny Lambourne who were off on a Scottish tour. The statistic needs no comment: it was simply that of all the National Nature Reserve land in Britain, three-quarters are in Scotland, mainly in the Highlands or out on the islands. And the writings that so appealed to us were Fraser Darling's *Natural History of the Highlands and Islands*—a model of how to describe a region and its wildlife; and *Mountain Flowers* by John Raven and Max Walters, a book that has sent many an aspiring plant-seeker northwards dreaming of treasures to be found on the mica-schists of Ben Lawers or the limestones of Inchnadamph.

May was yellowing the oaks as we drove up through southern Scotland. Everywhere the roadsides had enough oaks still along them to suggest that this was once a land of broad-leaved forest. But as you go north and the Grampians slowly position themselves along the skyline you begin to see more and more of the stately trees the British have always called Scotch fir or Scots pine despite the fact that *Pinus sylvestris* is native practically everywhere from Britain to the Himalayas. Still, this parochialism can be defended if you accept the view that the pines of Scotland differ enough from those of the Continent for them to deserve the status of a race apart. This being so, you may have even more respect for these grey-green foliaged, red-boughed giants that gather ever more frequently at the wayside. They are not just *Pinus sylvestris*, you remind yourself, but *Pinus sylvestris scotica*. And the crossbills you see flying out of them are equally, so some experts tell us, not just any crossbills, but Scottish crossbills. Likewise there is said to be something special about that other product of isolation, the Scottish crested tit. But the minute distinctions that separate these local races, though sport for a few scientists, are of little importance for the rest of us. For most people it is the moment and the place that matter: perhaps a crisp silent dawn in some high-placed forest when pines, tits and crossbills, though all so beautiful, are only part of a mountain and woodland wilderness.

Not even *Pinus sylvestris scotica* goes with you all the way to the north coast. By the time you have crossed into Sutherland and are still fifty miles from the sea, the world has changed again. The Scots pine is now mostly behind you (I speak not of forestry plantations) as the land spreads before you in a heart-stirring wilderness of loch and moorland where trees, genuine, self-planted, native trees are few. Such woods as you do see are nearly all of birch.

Once on the Sutherland coast you cease to think about trees altogether. Your thoughts turn to stark rocks that face the unkind arctic. Now life is full of gannets, fulmars, kittiwakes, mergansers and black guillemots. Genuine wild rock-doves—they breed all the year round even in these northern sea-caves—fly headlong round the cliffs. Pairs of grebe-like birds rise off the sea, circle to gain height, then fly directly inland, calling a loud 'kakakak' as they go: so you learn how red-throated divers feed daily in the sea and then return with a shout to breeding lakes miles inland. And anywhere along the wind-singing wires you see 'linnets' strung out in rows. These you should look at closely, for you may find something about them that is faintly unlinnet-like. Perhaps they seem more varied, more speckled, than the linnets you are used to, the breast perhaps more like a pipit's? So wait and watch. Sooner or later one of them will preen its back feathers and expose the strawberry-coloured rump that declares the birds not linnets but twites, which are a speciality of this coast. Soon you realize that their flocks are everywhere, feeding on the ground on weed seeds or dancing before you along the seaward slopes, often obligingly whispering 'twite' in your ear as they pass, as if they are anxious you do not mistake them for mere linnets.

If in your travels you have ever found yourself in late May or June on the limestone of north England or south Scotland, you will surely have seen one of Britain's most endearing little wild-flowers, the bird's-eye primrose, whose delicate leaves look flour-powdered underneath and give the plant its Latin name *Primula farinosa*. This jewel has a cousin that is almost its double but is only half the size. It grows, this tiny Scots primrose, all along the north coast of Scotland and in Orkney; and in those districts is not at all rare. Clearly *P. scotica* demands the smell of the sea. But I wonder why it has to be the sea of Sutherland, Caithness and Orkney and nowhere else in the world? Yes, it is as special as that.

You don't see the midnight sun from these wild cliffs. But it is a coast that can give you twenty-one hours of daylight in twenty-four if the month is June. It is also a coast of great winds that race across from the west or blast at you out of the north and east, winds that have helped the ocean to shatter the rocky coast of Sutherland into a ragged pattern of sea lochs, inlets and promontories so that the total shore-line is all of 600 miles.

Here and there you find the winds have done strange things with sand as well as with rock. At Torrisdale Bay, for instance, which is just west of the village called Bettyhill. This lovely cliff-girt inlet is sheltered both from east and west, but the north winds flow in freely from the open sea and rarely does a winter pass without at least six full-throated gales. Now it chances that opening into Torrisdale Bay are two parallel stream estuaries separated by a hill. These two streams, Borgie and Naver, between them bring down much silt to the bay. The silt spreads over the shore making a fine sandy beach; but sooner or later generous quantities of it get picked up by the gales and flung back against the hill. The result is a series of sand-dunes piled high up the rocks, dunes that have become known among botanists for the many wild plants that grow on this sand made lime-rich by crushed and powdered sea-shells.

The dunes that most of us know are bound together with marram grass. Yet here a principal sand-fixer is the mountain avens which makes generous cushions everywhere and, as on the slopes of Burren, seems a plant full of sea-longing. More likely what makes mountain avens and other arctic-alpines feel at home in such coastal sites is the combination of strong winds and persistent coolness they find there. So alongside the avens on these dunes, or on the rocks above, flourish treasures like purple saxifrage, moss campion, alpine bistort and yellow mountain saxifrage. Scots primrose is also here, for it lines the whole coast from Wrath to John o' Groats; and frog orchid that is always a joy; and moonwort, the little fern that so often is frog orchid's companion. Then a plant of rare distinction: the purple mountain milk-vetch that makes splashes of colour along an ancient beach raised fifty feet above the sea; and a near-rarity, the curious little thing called curved sedge whose roots creep far and send up forests of two-inch plants with round, dark-brown heads that are as conspicuous against the pale sand as currants on a bun.

These plant-rich dunes and the Pre-Cambrian rocks they are heaped against form the Invernaver National Nature Reserve, an oblong of country a mile across and going two miles back inland: big enough to include, besides the foreshore, a little upland world of its own, with peaty moorland and nesting greenshanks, crags with ring ouzels, lakelets with red-throated divers. And twites in plenty. Human memories too: along the raised beach, where the gales have partly torn aside the sands they once laid there, are exposed Bronze Age cairns and Iron Age hut circles and fort remains. Perhaps men lived continuously in this delectable if airy spot from prehistory through all the centuries till they were evicted at the brutal clearances of 1818. So ended an ancient community, the presumably Norse-originated township called, so simply, Lon.

At Invernaver you are near the centre of Britain's north coast. From there you can go east to explore infinite miles of heather moor and loch across inland Caithness. Here my sharpest memories are of the delicate yodelling of golden plover and the wild ululations of both black-throated and red-throated divers; and of seeing a pair of red-necked phalaropes paddling nonchalantly around the edge of a rush-fringed pool though I stood only a few feet away. But the country to the west is higher and more exciting. What land could not be that has in it two such striking peaks as Ben Loyal and Ben Hope and a stretch of vast cliffs like those from Durness to Wrath? This final, far north-east corner of Sutherland ought to be inviolable, a region—one of the last remaining in Britain—that should never be opened up with roads and exposed to the outrages of commerce, industry or the holiday trade. Yet what in fact are we doing to it? The military use part of the sea-cliffs (whose only rightful inhabitants are nesting seabirds) as a firing range. And is not lovely Loch Eriboll just the place to develop into a monstrous oil port?

Durness, one of the nearest villages to Cape Wrath, is a place of little renown, except among geologists. They all know it, at least by name, not as a village but as an outcrop of ancient limestone that begins on the north coast at Durness and stretches for many miles across country as a remarkably straight and narrow band aiming a little west of south and keeping close to a great fault-line called the Moine Thrust. The Durness limestone is as well known to naturalists as it is to geologists. As you can imagine, a great upthrust of limestone in a predominantly acid-soiled region means a real enrichment of the fauna and flora. In fact you don't need to be a naturalist to see the effect of the Durness limestone on the vegetation: the ridge stands up in many places as green and leafy hills in a world of sombre heather moor.

Botanists sniffing like truffle-hounds along this plant-rich limestone all come sooner or later to Inchnadamph, a name that is also written Innis-na-damph and means the Meadow (or the Island) of the Stag, for *innis*, like Welsh *ynys*, has both these meanings. In fact Inchnadamph is both a meadow and an island. It is an island of green sheep meadow in an ocean of heather, an oasis of sweet soil in a desert of acidity. It is a large island of which over three thousand acres are leased as a National Nature Reserve. But limestone as ancient as this does not make high mountains. If it ever did they have been eroded away long since. So Inchnadamph Reserve rises no higher than 1,700 feet and is a mere foot-hill for a handsome, Pre-Cambrian, crystalline mountain farther inland called Ben More Assynt which exceeds 3,200 feet, is the highest hill in Sutherland but has little botanical fame.

Inchnadamph has typical limestone features. There are caves that have yielded bones of cold-climate animals like lemming, reindeer, arctic fox, northern vole and northern lynx as well as traces of man perhaps as far back as Mesolithic time. There are pavement-like levels treacherous with deep crevices and there are sink-holes down which vanish streams that reappear farther on. It is up the stream called Traligill that many visitors find their way into the reserve. Its lower parts are leafy but as you come up clear of the trees you begin to see riches in the waterside rocks. Green spleenwort, of course, and shining leathery fronds of holly fern; yellow globe-flower and early purple orchids. Then at botanist's pace you climb gently onward, examining ledges at eye-level, peering into grikes or scrambling up clifflets, finding always something new: a rare couch-grass delightfully called Don's twitch (read in Raven and Walters the detective story of how they re-discovered it here); a distinguished sandwort, *Arenaria norvegica*; perhaps alpine enchanter's nightshade, twisted whitlow-grass, small white orchid or dark red helleborine. And along the upper rocks an unusual scrub, a mere nine or ten inches high, consisting of myrtle-leaved willow (*Salix myrsinites*). You come up to a loch called Mhaolach-coire, shallow-looking, about twenty acres. There are wigeon obviously breeding, as well as greenshanks and common sandpipers. Golden plovers sing all round and there is a piping of ring ouzels. Watch the surrounding hills for red deer; and the sky for golden eagles.

The slopes above the loch look decidedly moor-like and botani-cally uninviting. But as you climb you find the pale grey rock going up with you though beginning to get patchy. There is still plenty of avens and mountain everlasting and the ever delectable moss campion. Then you are off the limestone at last and into heather and bilberry. Grouse begin to bark and the view gets wider. But keep on looking for there are still good things to see: the choicer plants of the acid rocks—cloudberry with its showy white flowers that are followed by red bramble-like fruits; dwarf cornel, mountain azalea, black bearberry and, if you go high enough, least willow, which is very least indeed, for it is mostly under two inches high.

To anyone from the south, Inchnadamph, with its gorges, loch and heather moor, may seem a sizeable reserve. But it would be lost in one small corner of the 27,000 acres of its neighbouring reserve of Inverpolly whose toes are in the sea at Enard Bay and whose head is at Cul Mor (2,786 feet) six miles away. Another of its heights is Stac Polly (Stac Pollaidh), a sandstone boss that soars in isolation above Loch Lurgain and is an arresting peak even in a land where shapely heights like Suilven, Canisp and Quinag look at you from many an horizon. Inverpolly Reserve is full of relics of former days. There are woodlands of birch and hazel that are evident fragments of ancient forest. There are deer, wild cats, martens, eagles and ptarmigan. And even if there were none of these things it would still be a marvellous wilderness to go exploring in.

You certainly need the eye of faith to visualize any of the forests that once flourished in north-west Scotland. Especially the ashwoods that may have been the climax limestone vegetation of places like Inchnadamph. But it gets less difficult as you come south into the oakwood country. When you begin to see long narrow woods of sessile oak still clinging along the slopes of brown-earthed valleys, your mind's eye can imagine the far-spread oak forests of the Dark Ages. One such tilted oakwood faces you across Loch Maree at a place called Letterewe. It is a region where the last oakwoods were shaved off without thought or conscience by iron-smelters of the seventeenth and eighteenth centuries. Letterewe has the oldest iron-works site in Scotland and the oak-woods there now are probably nineteenth-century replantings—a commendable act of rehabilitation but they cover only a tiny fraction of the old oak forest area.

But it is not for their oaks that Loch Maree's banks are best known. As you follow the fair lochside from Gairloch you begin to see the steeps above you bristling not with oaks but venerable conifers. You are entering a Scots pine land, the magnificent, steeply sloping country that climbs from the loch-edge south-wards to Sgurr Ban (3,188 feet), one of the three summits of Beinn Eighe, a National Nature Reserve that covers some 10,000 superb acres of mountain and moorland. Here survives an ancient wood—Coille na Glas Leitire—just enough of it, but only just, to allow us to picture how this land probably looked when many of the skirts of the wet, western mountains were thick with pine forest triumphantly reproducing itself century by century. But we have to go far back to reach such splendid times. For maybe in the shadowy days of pre-history man was already at it, burning and hatcheting the first small clearings for his purposes. So it could be that Coille na Glas Leitire has been quite a small and isolated fragment for the past many hundreds of years. What is sure is that our century has practically finished it, the greatest trees going in the two World Wars, to be converted, many of them, into nothing better than ammunition boxes. Today the veteran survivors (they look every minute of 250 years old) stand bravely up their hillside with young pines springing happily about them, under the watchful care of the Nature Conservancy—a heart-lifting sight if you can believe that this example may inspire other landowners to exert themselves likewise in the cause of forest revival. But I fear regeneration may not be easy except in a few favoured spots. Destroy a forest in a land of great rains and steep slopes and you soon lose its ancient soils. On Beinn Eighe, once the trees had gone, the agents of erosion bit swiftly down to expose infertile sub-soils or bare rock. Now there is only heathy scrub, mats of weather-racked junipers and much lichen, moss and liverwort stretching for miles over the shoulders of the mountains.

Birds are few on Beinn Eighe's upper slopes but, with luck, you may see ptarmigan or eagle. As for animals, there are red deer and roe, wild cats and pine martens. But these two predators are among Britain's most elusive mammals and you can walk the hills for years and never meet with either. Perhaps your best chance is seeing one slip across the road in your car headlights. It was that way we reckoned we saw a wild cat one night alongside Loch Maree. But when we reported it next day to the assistant reserve warden he offered the chill comment that domestic cats gone wild were not uncommon thereabouts. He also told us that lately, for the entertainment of visitors, a hen's egg had been put each day in a litter bin at the lochside car-park at the bottom of the nature trail and that people watching quietly in their cars had often seen a marten come at dusk and help itself to the egg. So that evening we, too, waited in the car park till deep darkness fell. The same the next night also. But not a whisker of a marten, not an imagined tip of a marten's nose did any of us see. Not that I expected to. I have searched so hard for martens in so many places without success I now almost classify them with the Yeti and Loch Ness Monster.

Perhaps you will say it is right that shy wild animals should remain shy and wild; and that it would be wrong if hawks settled tamely on our heads as a Galapagos hawk once perched on Darwin's. But I wonder if we haven't gone rather too far in our repression of some animals? Is it possible that we have driven some of the more sensitive creatures beyond the limits of mere shyness; that we have over-persecuted and they have over-retreated and now lead lives of such desperate withdrawal that they find it very difficult psychologically to make a come-back even when harassment has long ceased and conditions seem to favour their revival? How else explain why a species like the marten remains so exceedingly rare even in most of the wildest parts of the British Isles? So it was good to know that the martens of Beinn Eighe can learn to come for eggs in a litter bin; and to hear that somewhere in the Highlands a patient marten-wooer even has one that regularly comes to his house for food in the evening, entering a drawing-room by way of the french windows!

Twenty miles south-west of Beinn Eighe you pick up the Durness limestone again as you get near Loch Kishorn. As you come down the valley towards the loch on the road from Shieldaig you have a sandstone ridge up on your right; but the slope on your left climbs gently away as limestone. And though at Inchna-damph the original ash forest has totally gone, here above Loch Kishorn it lingers on but only as the most wretched collection of trees you ever saw—old, battered, degenerate and pitifully few. And under them no trace of undergrowth and hardly any flowering plants. Nothing but the sheep-ravaged turf.

But do not turn away in sadness from this the most northerly ashwood surviving in Britain. For it is now a National Nature Reserve and has its hopeful side. Go through the trees a little way and you come to where a few acres of formerly open ground have been enclosed by the Nature Conservancy to find out what would happen if grazing were excluded. So for the first time in centuries a portion of Rassal Wood was rescued from the merciless incisors of rabbits, sheep and cattle. The result has been quite wonderful.

Outside the fence the uninteresting close-nibbled sward; but everywhere inside is a delightfully varied, green world gay with saplings of ash, hazel and bird cherry. And below them a rejoicing of primroses, anemones, herb robert, water avens, bluebells and tall grasses. Not a square foot that doesn't seem to be bursting to produce some choice plant after so long a history of frustration. So although most of Rassal Wood is dying on its feet, a part at least has been saved on the stroke of midnight. I pray that some-how the means will be found to fence in far more and re-create a truly generous stretch of the forest that was, and that it will never again be given back to the sheep which, after all, have a very generous stake in the rest of Scotland.

Though the Scots have not yet gone in officially for national parks you might be excused for assuming they possess in effect at least one when you realize the extent of the Cairngorms National Nature Reserve and see, next-door to it, the crowds motoring up the spectacular road from Loch Morlich to 2,100 feet, then getting another leg-up by chair-lift on to the shoulders of Cairn Gorm itself. Once up there they have easy access to a very special area of Britain, our greatest tract of country over 3,000 feet, an un-peopled wilderness of slopes and screes that lead you up past crags, moraines, corries, torrents, waterfalls, high-placed lochs and moorlands, to exposed granitic summits at over 4,000 feet.

Admitted, from a distance the Cairngorms can be a disappoint-ment if you go expecting to find shapely peaks towering along the horizon. For what you see from most angles is a rather unexciting moorland mass. The truth about the Cairngorms is that they were once a plateau; and from a distance a plateau they still appear to be because their summits, relics of the old plateau surface, are so wide and flattish-topped. It is not until you are in the heart of the region and see the deep passes, glens and crag-surrounded cwms created by the dissolution of vast quantities of softer rocks that you realize what a much more splendid world lies within these mountains than you'd ever guess from outside.

In one or two famous hollows on Braeriach and Ben Macdhui, two of the Cairngorms' summits, you can find snow that is almost perpetual. Even more enduring relics of the Ice Age are certain

mountaintop insects, birds and plants extremely worthy of conservation. But far better than trying to protect individual species
is the safeguarding of the whole region, much of whose pristine
ecology is intact to a degree enjoyed by very few other parts of
Britain. The uplands, for instance, still have red deer in their
hundreds. The pinewoods harbour many groups of roe. There are
wild cats (though as everywhere very hard to find), mountain
hares and red squirrels. Crossbills, crested tits, siskins and caper-
caillies are all numerous in the forests. The high places have
eagles, greenshanks, snow buntings, ptarmigans and dotterels. Up
there the botanist finds good plants like Scottish asphodel,
alpine willow-herb, alpine speedwell, Scottish rush, spiked woodrush, interrupted clubmoss, myrtle-leaved willow and half a
dozen rare ones best not advertized. And for the tree enthusiast
there are the beautiful pines of Rothiemurchus and Glen More.

What of the future of the Cairngorms? There are, I know, some
who see with horror how the highest tops are now opened wide
to tourism. Can the rarer, more sensitive animals, birds and plants
survive such an impact? At first sight it may seem almost inevitable that some of them, so precariously surviving here in the
mountain solitudes, must now finally give up. Yet though things
may not look promising, it could be that we are going to see some
splendid acts of conservation in this great nature reserve where so
much is at stake and where so many interests are trying to work
together in one of the biggest exercises in multiple land-use and
countryside protection in all Britain. The landowners, the Nature
Conservancy Council, the County Councils, the National Trust
for Scotland, the Forestry Commission, the Cairngorms Winter
Sports Development Board, the Scottish Council of Physical
Recreation, the thousands of visitors: all have a part to play, a
wise and co-operative part, in keeping the Cairngorms as they are
—a wilderness. But a wilderness that will be enjoyed by many. Is
this a totally ridiculous notion? Wilderness plus people equals
what? This is the equation that has to be solved by those to whose
care these magnificent Cairngorms are entrusted. One thing is
certain: some extremely testing conservation problems will stretch
far into the future.

If I have mentioned only a few of Scotland's many National Nature Reserves it is because most are unknown to me. I would love to have had time to see and write about them all—and those of north England too. But there is one delicious Yorkshire reserve that lay on our way back from Scotland. I mean the National Nature Reserve on Ingleborough called Colt Park Wood, an ashwood on limestone pavement. At Ingleborough you find a landscape very like that of the Burren—round-capped hills that come down in even steps of almost bare, pale rock. There are rare plants in Colt Park Wood but, as on the Burren, it is the luxuriant show of commoners that makes the place so totally a delight. Botanically speaking one of the most attractive woods in Britain, it is also one of the most dangerous. In limestone pavement cracks are everywhere: but in Colt Park Wood they are not only deep and wide (some you won't jump across) but also are often bushed over with vegetation that grows quite unimpeded, the place being far too hazardous to allow any grazing. So be warned.

Go if you can in spring when the bird cherries hang their white flowers all through the wood and the best of the wildflowers are in bloom. You will be struck first, I think, by a contrast: all round stretch bleak, harassed-looking, over-nibbled sheep lands, all quite lacking in promise for the eager plant-seeker. Then you come under the trees of Colt Park as to an oasis in an unkind land. There you find green coolness and a joyousness of scents and colours. Under low leafy branches great spreads of the healthiest red campion you ever saw, white sheets of wild garlic, beds yellow with globe flowers, white billows of mossy saxifrage. You look down into the wide crevices at forests of hartstongue fern and hard shieldfern, lovely white patches of woodruff, elegant specimens of wall lettuce. Or you lower yourself gingerly down into one of those generous grikes and look at your plants the ideal way —at eye-level. Now you find the smaller treasures: green spleenwort, brittle bladder fern, moonwort, moschatel, fingered saxifrage, early purple orchid, hairy rockcress, water avens and shining cranesbill.

The plants I have mentioned are only a few of the total. You could go on adding common showy species like valerian, crosswort, lady's bedstraw, rock-rose and meadowsweet, and then rather more exclusive kinds like goldilocks, angular Solomon's seal, melancholy thistle, giant bellflower, wood cranesbill, herb Paris and lily of the valley. And that speciality of northern England, the baneberry, with its massed plumes of white flowers that are followed by shining black berries. Surrounded by such delights you may wonder if English limestone anywhere has expressed itself in flowers more successfully than in this little wood of Colt Park. Quite properly such a choice spot has to be safeguarded. It is therefore necessary, before going to Colt Park, to get a permit from the Nature Conservancy Council.

9. The Wilder Face of Wales

It would be fascinating sometime to have the privilege of conducting a party of foreign conservationists round Wales, or rather to those parts of Wales that most appeal to me, especially the wilder places where the natural world still survives, however precariously. But where to begin? First impressions of a country are important and I would not wish my visitors to reach Wales along some dispiriting main road from the east. The real Wales for me is the Wales that has its feet in the western sea, a land that meets the ocean with cliffs of ancient rock, then builds up quickly into robust moorlands and mountains. I would therefore try to arrange for my guests to arrive by ship at Holyhead so that their first view of Wales could be of a green sea bursting in whiteness along Anglesey's cliffs. And their first touch of Wales would be when their feet step off the ferry on to the quartzite of Holyhead's long breakwater. Coming into the town they would see the shoreline quarries from which this crystalline rock was cut. And above they would look up to Holyhead Mountain whose Pre-Cambrian rocks, catching the sun, are so pale they can seem like snow. For in all Wales there is no light more brilliant than that which falls on Anglesey or on the peninsulas north and south of Cardigan Bay.

While my visitors' thoughts were still on rocks I would show them how the Romans used local stone to build their wall that still stands strong and high by Holyhead's church of St. Cybi. They would see how clearly some of these stones show in miniature the extremely twisted strata whose tortures are visible on a huge scale in the near-by cliffs. They tell of pressures that a long time ago flowed through the earth from the south-east, slowly rumpling the rocks into parallel ridges and troughs that ran from north-east to south-west, a structure that is still significant in the landscape of Wales and unmistakable in Anglesey itself.

From Holyhead we would find a cliff path to lift us quickly through yellow gorse and pallid quartzite to the breezy headland of North Stack, then round and up to Anglesey's highest point, the summit called Caer y Twr where the Iron Age placed a walled enclosure that is still traceable. But with rocks of hard, sharp silica sticking up everywhere like teeth this was a comfortless perch and inevitably there is scant sign of settled habitation. Iron Age forts are almost all great viewpoints and from Caer y Twr you have one of the classic prospects of Wales. Standing up here on what, geologically speaking, are the basement rocks of Wales, you look east across a very ancient world: for Anglesey, despite more recent sediments that lie on the surface here and there, is outstandingly a land of Pre-Cambrian rocks that continue under Afon Menai (to give the strait its Welsh name), re-appear briefly on the other side around Bangor, then are lost deep under the Cambrian and Ordovician rocks of Snowdonia whose mountains are the heart-lifting background of this view from Caer y Twr.

In the hope of seeing choughs, sea-birds or seals we would go down through the rocks to South Stack. And if it were spring or early summer the steep places everywhere would be coloured and fragrant with flowers—ample cushions of thrift and kidney vetch, scurvy grass and birdsfoot trefoil, sea campion and thyme. I doubt if in all Britain there exists a gayer show of wild blossom than is found along slopes above the sea. Add to these delights the sharp sneeze of a red-beaked, red-legged, black-plumaged chough as he comes bouncing down the sea wind; and the whirring flight of puffins, guillemots or razorbills climbing the air to their nesting ledges. Or simply be satisfied with the unique cliffs themselves, these totally primal rock faces that speak so eloquently of the tensions that for ever wrack and harass the earth. Yet it is these torments that have made the world beautiful, raising mountains, carving valleys, shaping coastlines. With which thought I would lead my friends, however reluctant they might be to quit the glories of South Stack, away to Cemlyn Bay.

Cemlyn, with its simple arc of pebble beach narrowly separating restless sea from placid lagoon; Cemlyn, with its terns and summer flowers, is altogether delightful. And it is a nature reserve. But soon or late my companions must raise their eyes, must look out to sea, must point to the vast, squat, solid, ugly Thing that has been built on the headland two miles distant. For this is what we, the long-civilized British, have done. This is the twentieth century's contribution to Anglesey, mother of Wales. Here in the fullest consciousness of what we were doing, we chose to bring an atomic power station to pollute a stretch of cliffs and bays and headlands that through all previous centuries of time had survived in faultless beauty. And presumably when the power station has become a redundant and dangerous hulk the twenty-first century will have to spend vast energy and money burying it deep in concrete. And that concrete will only be got by making a scar on somebody's landscape. No, the next century will not thank us for Wylfa power station any more than we love the nineteenth for the wreck of Parys Mountain near by. But because seeing the worst helps us to appreciate the best I would take my party up to Parys to look down into that dreadful copper-mining hole (with its more recent contribution of abandoned cars and other rubbish) which for squalor is equal to anything in the lower Swansea valley, the place usually acclaimed as man's greatest achievement so far in the degradation of Welsh landscape.

After Parys we would need cheering up. So where better to go than Cors Goch, a charming little fenland near Benllech? Here a wealth of distinguished marsh plants flourish on the site of a former lake, plants that love the sweet water draining off the limestone escarpment under which the fen shelters. A rare little wilderness to find surviving into our time in the lowlands of Wales, a place of peace and much charm and, praise be, it is a reserve of the North Wales Naturalists' Trust. The limestone goes on in splendour along the coast to the east, making ever greater cliffs that end at the white promontory of Penmon. On the way you pass Bwrdd Arthur, a wide, high, flowery platform that in the Iron Age was a hillfort, some of whose wall-footings are still clear to see. The name means 'Arthur's Table' and a table it certainly is, but we can guess that the name Arthur was supplied by some Dark Age or later romancer. For the story-tellers of those days loved to put their tales into local settings. To make up interesting place names was clearly part of their fun; and the map of Wales is still strewn with the products of their fertile inventiveness.

Not only Bwrdd Arthur is bright with limestone flowers. They adorn and enrich this whole north-east corner of Anglesey: rock-roses, marjoram, blood-red cranesbill, salad burnet, choice orchids and many other colourful and scented herbs—delights that you will seek in vain on the acid soils so dominant elsewhere in north Wales. Penmon has many attractions: cliffs, sea-birds, a former deer park, ancient stones, views of Puffin Island, priory ruins, a well-preserved dovecote of some history. But what I would especially want my visitors to see is the delicately carved (though now very worn) cross that dates from about the year A.D. 1000, so unexpected a treasure to find, far from houses, out among the fields behind the cliffs. Why was it set up there in that lonely place? Did it mark a burial of someone now forgotten? Did it stand along a road now lost? Outside a chapel now gone? Whatever the reasons it is a most encouraging symbol for conservationists when you think how it has stood there unguarded over nine hundred years, yet could have been destroyed at any time by vandals in only a few minutes.

From Penmon we would go south to Llanddwyn Island. It would be a return to the Pre-Cambrian rocks, not in the form of cliffs as at South Stack but as the broken stumps of what may have been cliffs at some remote time and are now merely wave-washed reefs and islets, worn yet still healthy teeth that have gone on defying the elements after more rotten material has quite dissolved away. Over the water we might see shags, cormorants, terns; on the land the rock sea-lavender, sea bindweed, blood-red cranesbill and other delights. Next door to Llanddwyn lie the 1,500 acres of Newborough Warren that are a National Nature Reserve. There we would spend happy hours botanizing in those lovely dunes so rich in flowers. But there is a shadow close by, the dark shadow of the conifer plantations that have spread half across this dune-land annihilating the native flora and fauna which, before our conifer-crazed age, had lived there for centuries. Is it too naïve to hope that more enlightened days are coming now that the Forestry Commission (see its Booklet 29—*Wildlife Conservation in Woodlands*) has at last come round to the idea of breaking into the conifer blanket, if only a little, in the interests of nature? A spokesman of theirs has claimed lately that the Forestry Commission has 'a fine record in conservation'. But among the evidence for this he cites the introduction of aliens such as Carolina duck and Reeves pheasant. I think most naturalists in Wales will be more convinced of the Forestry Commission's conversion to real conservation when it has made a start by, say, clearing a couple of hundred acres at Newborough Warren, so giving us back our lost dune hollows and marshes once so full of flowers and butterflies.

Newborough Warren has spectacular views east and south. All along the east, behind a foreground of near-white sand and pale green marram grass, you see the exciting line of 'Snowdon and all his sons', to revive an eighteenth-century phrase of Thomas Pennant. The south view is across the sea, and beyond it another high and undulating mountain line built up of rocks as ancient as those of Anglesey, the Pre-Cambrian rocks of the peninsula of Lleyn (as the English spell it) or Llŷn (as the Welsh have it) or Lene (as Leland wrote it when he came there in the sixteenth century). 'Al Lene', he noted tersely, 'is as it were a pointe into the se.' He was correct of course but I doubt if he made the discovery till he got right out to the end. Unless maybe he climbed Yr Eifl or some such height and saw how the hills diminished all the way along the peninsula and how the seas on each side grew closer to each other. But no, I don't somehow see Leland climbing Yr Eifl. Leland was an antiquary, a poker about among church plate and monastic treasures, not a mountaineer. But he was observant. Making his slow way down Lleyn he must often have stopped his horse to look at the view and could hardly have failed to note, as the land grew more treeless and rocky, the wind fresher and the sky wider, that the sea was closing in on him.

So, perhaps, he came to the end, reached the last village, Aberdaron, with its ancient shore-line church, went on into the west up the hill beyond and came out on to one of Britain's finest headlands, Braich y Pwll. If he had not been sure before, it came home to him now, with only the ocean before him, that 'Al Lene' certainly is 'a pointe into the se'. But probably he didn't look out to sea very long, not straight out into the empty west. Not many people do, from Braich y Pwll, unless they are dedicated sea-watchers. (Sea-watchers, in case you don't know are bird-watchers with a self-torturing mania for burning their eyes out by staring hour after hour through binoculars or telescopes at often unidentifiable sea-birds flying past miles out over the ocean.) No, people don't normally look west from Braich y Pwll because always the eye comes round south to the island that sits out in the glinting sea two miles away, the final broken-off bit of the Pre-Cambrian rocks, Bardsey, most cherished of Welsh islands.

I would greatly wish to take my friends to Bardsey. But we would have to choose our day. Bardsey Sound is a water where winds and tides enjoy an almost daily battle. And all down the ages people who wished to cross (and they have been many) have stood frustrated on the storm-washed headland holding out their hands in longing for the farther shore and doubting if that dangerous sea could ever befriend them. But at last—in two days or two weeks—the sea falls calm, you get into an open boat in the little cliff-girt, stony cove called Porth Meudwy, and off you go just as thousands of pilgrims went before you through all the Middle Ages. You have an engine, they had sails, that is the only difference. Except that their sails were probably more dependable than your engine.

Bardsey looks forbidding as you approach it like this, from the north-east. Your boat comes in under long, grassy slopes that break off into clifflets at the bottom. You look up the short-turfed mountainside and all you see is rocks, gorse, bracken, gulls and precariously grazing sheep. Not easy for your companions to believe they will find a comfortable bed that night. The boat turns south, keeping what seems dangerously close to the rocks to get out of the strong current. Razorbills dive off their nesting ledges and come whirring just over your head, though why they fly to greet you like this I have never understood. But I always enjoy

A high park in east Africa. *Above (a)*, the volcanic Mount Meru whose southern slopes are the setting for Arusha National Park, Tanzania. *Right (b)*, Desmond Vesey-FitzGerald who, until his death in 1974, was the park's chief scientific officer

10 *Above* (*a*), Ngurdoto Crater in Arusha National Park, Tanzania. The crater floor, which is completely forest-encircled, is a plain whose darker areas are swampy. Many elephants, buffaloes and rhinos graze in this crater. *Left* (*b*), one of the colobus monkeys that live in the forests

11 *Top right* (*a*), Ramsey Sound on the south Wales coast near St. David's, looking from Ramsey Island, an R.S.P.B. reserve, to the mainland. The rising tide flows north through a reef known as the Bitches. *Bottom right* (*b*), grey seals are especially numerous round Ramsey's rocky coast

12 Bird protection in Wales. *Top* (*a*) a red kite. Breeding in Britain in Wales only, the kite has gradually increased in recent years through careful protection organized by the Kite Committee. *Bottom* (*b*), the Kite Committee in 1964. Left to right: R. S. Thomas, Peter Panting, Penny Condry, Col. Morrey Salmon, T. A. W. Davis, Mrs. I. M. Vaughan, R. H. Baillie, William Condry, Capt. H. R. H. Vaughan, Dr. Clifford Fenn. In more recent years kite protection has become a joint responsibility of the R.S.P.B. and the Nature Conservancy Council

13 National Nature Reserves in Scotland. *Top* (*a*), Inchnadamph, showing pale limestone outcrops in dark peaty moorland. *Centre* (*b*), Beinn Eighe (3,309 feet), highest point of the Beinn Eighe reserve. *Bottom* (*c*), the corries of Braeriach in the Cairngorms from Rothiemurchus Forest

14 Birdwatchers' island. *Top* (*a*), Bardsey Island (Ynys Enlli), two miles off the tip of the Lleyn Peninsula, is well known for its migrant birds. *Bottom* (*b*), the lighthouse with its brilliant white flashing beam attracts passing birds many of which kill themselves by crashing into the tower. On a bad night (usually low cloud or rain) hundreds of birds of many kinds may die

15   Garden birds at Ynys Edwin. *Top left* (*a*), a pair of pied fly-catchers at their box on a window ledge. *Top right* (*b*), a cock red-start at a nest box. *Bottom* (*c*), tree pipits were among the first to nest in the newly created garden

16   Ynys-hir R.S.P.B. reserve on the Dyfi estuary. *Top* (*a*), a view of the reserve with the hills of Snowdonia beyond. *Bottom* (*b*), Venture Scouts erecting a bird-watching hide on the bank of the estuary

this intimate salute from these birds of the ocean that most other times treat man with total indifference.

Rounding a point you turn into a landing place through a gap amid seaweed-covered rocks. And the world changes. Cliffs, rocks, seaweed, sea-birds—these give place to a scene of quiet fields and scattered farms, a tranquil, pastoral world you would never suspect existed, so hidden is it as your boat comes across the sound. Ashore you follow a rough road that climbs gently past the first house, then a former schoolroom, then a few more houses till, at the north end of the island, you reach the unimposing abbey ruins. Here, a final cluster of houses, a chapel and farm buildings—relics of a people who have gone, their graves left behind in the burial ground by the abbey. Some of the stones tell their names. But many of the graves are ancient and marked only by crude boulders. Most of the houses are of the same age and style (for there was a vigorous rebuilding by the owner, Lord Newborough, in the late nineteenth century) and only one old-style cottage is left to speak of Bardsey's past. But the pattern of little fields persists and should never be interfered with: for as the years go by it is certain to be increasingly valued as a rare survival of old farming ways. You see it spread out below you as you climb up Bardsey Mountain. And if you search around those small fields you will, just here and there, come upon flat rectangles in the turf where stood cottages now almost gone from human memory.

Bardsey then is far more habitable than it looks from the mainland. Behind the hump of its gorsy hill you discover an unexpected, quite fertile land that slopes gently to the shore. The sea is intimately with you. All day you look at it. You listen to it at night in bed. Even in calm weather it murmurs on the little beach called Solfach and speaks softly along all the rocks. Night especially is the time to hear the seals moaning off-shore, lying out on the half-tide rocks. And only at night do you hear Bardsey's wildest sound, the sobbing and shrieking of hundreds of shearwaters arriving from the ocean to their secretive nests inside field walls, down rabbit holes or in burrows which they dig into the grassy slopes with sharp claws.

K

Calm or stormy, summer or winter, there is one ingredient common to every Bardsey night. Tirelessly from dusk till dawn the lighthouse sends out its blinding, revolving white flashes. One, two, three, four, five—they swing remorselessly round. A black pause of ten seconds and they are at you again. And while they mean comfort to ships at sea they bring death to migrant birds. Not on clear nights of star or moon; for then the birds pass high and safely over. But in bad weather there may be disaster. Perhaps the birds set off at dusk from some place where the sky is clear, enabling them to navigate without fault. If, nearing Bardsey, they run into murk or rain they are forced to fly low, seeking landmarks. It is then they feel the pull of the lighthouse. You can hear them as soon as you go out of doors—the thin notes that some migrating birds send to each other through the darkness. The notes increase the nearer you get to the lighthouse and soon you begin to see an occasional bird shining a moment in these beams that swing round like the spokes of a wheel. When you get to the lighthouse and look straight up you see a multitude of birds swirling round in the brilliant white paths of light, some low down and large, others so high they look like sparks above a fire. And now the air is full of birds' cries, perhaps of redwings, blackbirds and starlings; and often there is the *crump* of those who, totally dazzled, crash into the lighthouse tower to fall fluttering and broken to the ground.

If my companions wanted to know how long these shocking casualties have been going on I would have to admit the answer could be ever since the lighthouse was built in 1821 and that they have no doubt got worse as the power of the light has increased. The question might well arise: how can we make such a fuss about the French killing migrant birds while we allow our lighthouses to go on with this sort of slaughter. (On the night of 29–30 August 1968 about 585 perished at Bardsey light, including 111 grasshopper warblers, 117 sedge warblers, 153 willow warblers and 183 whitethroats.) It would be far from true to say that no attempt has been made to reduce the casualties. The R.S.P.B. years ago provided rails round the top of the tower for birds to rest on; later, in the hope that birds would see and avoid it, the

Society supplied lamps to floodlight the tower and has made grants towards research into the problem. And successive wardens and helpers at the bird observatory have put in endless hours, often in appalling midnight weather, trying to help the victims, some of which have recovered after a night's rest. But the fact remains that the casualties continue and the lighthouse cats grow fat. It looks as if the only improvement possible is an alteration in the nature of the light. Lighthouses, after all, need not kill birds. There are plenty that are perfectly harmless. So is it not time the Elder Brethren of Trinity House woke up to the idea of altering conditions at Bardsey and other dangerous lights?

Bird-watchers and small migrant birds have one thing in common: both love islands, just for short visits. So both come to Bardsey in spring when the birds are passing north from Africa to breed in the arctic; and again in autumn when the birds are returning. On a good day at these seasons the island's fields and hedges can for a while be alive with warblers, flycatchers, finches, especially if easterly breezes are wafting these little migrants away from their more usual fly-ways across the Continent. In these promising conditions we might get a real scoop on Bardsey: the sight of some eastern species like a yellow-browed warbler, a greenish warbler or a red-breasted flycatcher. But more likely such halcyon weather will soon be nudged away by the next depression that fetches a gale of wind and rain from far down the Atlantic. Not much for us to do then but crouch in the shelter of a rock and watch the sea. But it needn't be an empty sea. For even tempests have their rewards for bird-watchers and can bring a marvellous fly-past of birds quite close inshore. Guillemots, razorbills, puffins scurrying on short wings, often using the deep green valleys between the rollers to get down out of the wind. Others, the long-winged ones, the shearwaters, gannets and kittiwakes, needing no shelter, glide buoyantly on, sliding easily forwards as they tack across the gale. To see a dozen guillemots go scurrying by is nothing. It is when you have sat there day after day and watched hundreds of such parties pressing on down the face of the ocean, all on exactly the same purposeful line, that you begin to realize you are witnessing a truly vast migration.

There are other things to see from these rocks. Very tame purple sandpipers and turnstones clamber near you, searching the wet seaweed just above wave-wash level. Rock pipits (ever wary) flit and shriek among the crevices. Even here in the throat of the storm a wren's song suddenly comes through the boom and splash of the breakers. For Bardsey is an island of wrens: they feed in the sea caverns and among the lichen-yellow rocks of the shore as they feed all through the gorse and bracken of the mountain and in the hedges round every field. And there are the seals that so unexpectedly raise a head from the heaving water and watch you without fear, without much emotion of any sort, it seems; just staring at you full of curiosity until you feel mildly discomforted. You begin to understand seal folklore and why there is a wide-spread belief that seals were once people. I know of no wild creatures whose look is so personal, as if they really are turning over philosophical ideas about you. Then they tire of you and dive deep and in a few minutes maybe one of them brings up a writhing conger and you have to sit and watch the wretched fish die a slow death while played with in the seal's great teeth. Slowly he chews great red and raw pieces out of it, little morsels floating away to be picked up by neatly diving kittiwakes who have gathered to the feast.

And all the while the wind roars, the breakers rage against the flood tide and foam goes away in white straggling lines across the green and tossing sea. On each side of you, sheltering as best you can in the lee of your rock, great waves beat unceasingly up the cliffs and fall cascading back. But they are nothing to the seas that every now and then go bursting white up and over Carreg Ddu, a mid-sea rock two miles north. The same at the end of the main-land, Braich y Pwll, the ultimate 'pointe into the se': there even huger seas explode into spray that falls slowly back from a height of a hundred feet or more. Yes, I'm sure my friends would enjoy being stormbound on Ynys Enlli, to give the island its ancient name.

From Bardsey Mountain you look to the peaks of Yr Eifl and Snowdonia grouped distantly in the east. But which to select to take my companions to? Snowdon itself, for a start, to show them what griefs and problems a railway brings to a mountain. Then, for contrast, the wild, high ridges of the Carneddau that are still remote and peaceful, as mountains should be. We would climb also one or two of the many smaller heights—those that do not reach 3,000 feet but which include in their number some of the best-loved hills of Wales—Moel Hebog, Cnicht, Moelwyn, Siabod, Rhinog, Diffwys, Cadair Idris, Aran Fawddwy, Arennig and so many more. I would certainly include Yr Eifl in my itinerary. Yr Eifl (which translates as The Fork) whose three granite prongs rise sharp behind the coast a few miles south-west of Caernarfon. From up there, more clearly than from any other viewpoint, we would see the shape of north-west Wales: how Anglesey lies low and separate across the water in the north; how Lleyn tails away into the south-west as a line of diminishing hills; how Cardigan Bay curves firmly away on the south under the lively shapes of Rhinog and Cadair Idris; how, close on the east, tower the greater peaks of Snowdonia. But Yr Eifl has one further claim to distinction: from its highest point you look down, as if from an aircraft, on one of the archaeological treasures of Wales. For there on a hill top 250 feet below you and half a mile distant is spread Tre'r Ceiri (Giants' Town), a unique community of Iron Age hut circles, hut semi-circles, hut squares and hut oblongs, about a hundred and fifty of them, crowded into five acres and surrounded by a still massive bank of stones which, when fresh from the hands of its builders, must have been a first-class bit of drystone walling. Even today, after the dilapidations and robberies of seventeen centuries, you can still, in places, see the original structure: an outer high wall protecting a sentry walk on the inside. Elsewhere in Wales, though hill-forts are many, there is nothing like Tre'r Ceiri, nothing like this wealth of hut remains (they even continue down some of the slopes outside the city walls), no place that hints so convincingly of what life may have been like in the Roman-British time.

My visitors would, I think, be interested to see the Great Orme. This famous Orme (the name is Viking) is a marvellous chunk of hard, sheer-sided limestone, 679 feet high, that thrusts itself a couple of miles into the sea and has Llandudno crouching below, grateful for a little shelter from the north-west winds. What is fascinating about the Orme is the double part it manages to play. Its summit plateau is thronged in summer like some park in the middle of a city: for people go up there by road, by tramway and by cable car. And yet in places, full of steep cliffs, there is almost a wilderness atmosphere with so many sea-birds nesting on the ledges and so many wildflowers springing in the turf. For by rare good fortune the requirements of man on the Orme are on the whole different from those of nature.

So I would show my friends the Great Orme cliffs, the pale crags where herring gulls, kittiwakes, fulmars, shags and others have their nests; and where juniper, wild cabbage, dark red helleborine and a unique cotoneaster (*Cotoneaster integerrimus*) flourish in defiance of the gales. Then to scrub-covered slopes to seek the Nottingham catchfly which opens its delicately fragrant blooms at night to attract the moths, then carefully furls its petals as daylight broadens. A fine composite, the spotted catsear, also flourishes here among rocks and bushes, its purple-blotched hairy leaves and two-inch yellow flower-discs making it an endearing plant to find. These are spring flowers. Among summer joys are the blue flowers of the spiked speedwell and the yellow heads of what in Wales is a real rarity, the buttercup called goldilocks. Perhaps such problems as do face nature on the Orme are those that affect the turf flowers of the summit. Hoary rock-rose, vernal squill, horseshoe vetch, spring cinquefoil, spring sandwort: these are treasures of May and June which are fading to brownness and seed by the time the summer crowds arrive. Even so the ever increasing trampling of feet must wear them away at last and there seems a strong case for a few areas to be protected.

For a contrast with sea-girt limestone we would go farther east to the acid-soiled hills of Clwyd which, though rapidly losing their wildness as more and more people invade, are still a lovely twenty miles of uplands and, for lovers of past things, are note worthy for their line of six high-placed hill-forts that stride the country from north to south. I would especially wish my party to see Penycloddiau whose summit banks enclose the largest single hill-fort in Wales. Not that it is the revealing place that Tre'r Ceiri is, for it is lacking in hut remains. But it is high, wide, breezy and far-seeing. In fact few places in Wales give you a better Iron Age view of the world.

Somewhere on the north Welsh uplands we would seek out a few of the ancient trackways that still go so full of purpose across the land. They marked the trade routes of Bronze Age man. They led from fort to fort in the Iron Age. They guided man through the Dark Ages. They connected medieval abbeys and towns. And they remained in continual use till the threshold of our time. Nor have we abandoned them: it is simply that we use them not for business but for pleasure. What better paths exist anywhere than those that cross the high moorland of Berwyn, paths such as Ffordd Saeson and Ffordd Gam Elin, that were surely links between the north-west Wales and the south-east England of prehistory?

From Berwyn we would move south, south of Welshpool and the Severn, to other hills with other ancient routes. The one that goes south-west along the top of Long Mountain, for instance, which has all the feel of a Roman road as it keeps to the top of the ridge and heads so directly for their camp at Forden. When it drops down the western end of the hill it passes close to a spot that would especially intrigue any Americans I might have in my party. I mean that prize exhibit of the Royal Forestry Society, the redwood grove at Leighton. Some of my visitors may have seen redwoods growing in their native soil on the mountain slopes of California where these conifers (*Sequoia sempervirens*) formerly made wonderful forests full of trees of immense size and antiquity until man came and exploited them with the utmost greed and wastefulness. Planted on Long Mountain in the mid nineteenth century, the redwoods have found fertile ground (this part of Wales was once renowned for oaks of vast size) and now the sequoias contain more timber to the acre than any other woodland in Britain. Admittedly, it is anything but a wild spot, this plantation, but an inspiring sight all the same, not only to foresters but to all who have respect for majestic trees. If that other western American, the Sitka spruce, now planted so multitudinously in Britain, were also going to be given the chance of making forests of giant trees (as it is perfectly capable of doing) then conservationists might be less unhappy with it. Instead the spruces are doomed under present forest policy to be clear-felled when mere infants of forty-five or fifty and so never escape from the dark, depressing stage of being closely crowded poles and little else.

From Long Mountain, still in pursuit of wide-skied uplands, it would be a natural step to Kerry Hill. Here we would find more hints of man's far past, particularly the long-distance, east-west routes that linked England and Wales and which are still straddled by dykes built on each side of them as road-blocks against the Welsh (or against the English?). Shadowy history, all this, but appealing with the simple directness of history on the ground, history far from libraries. But if you find little interest in the past it hardly matters as long as you enjoy being up on these high places where the wind blows in the grass and larks sing every-where and the view goes far across this splendid borderland.

From Kerry Hill we would go down with the Teme which hereabouts is the boundary between Wales and England. And a few miles before Knighton at Llanfair Waterdine (typical border place-name mix-up) we would take to the hills again, this time some hills just in England, in the Forest of Clun. So we would come up to a high crest called Spoad Hill and from above 1,300 feet would see far lands east of Wales, would look across to Stiperstones and Long Mynd and all the other heights that make up that muscular half of Shropshire. Spoad Hill would give us more than uplifting views. It would bring us to a bank and a ditch of immense significance for the Welshness of Wales. Up here on these treeless sheepwalks we would find Offa's Dyke at its best, swinging itself up the slopes to vanish over distant shoulders. I hope my friends would like to consider the long duration of this simple monument. Throw up a bank of earth, as Offa did, leave it to turf over and you have created something that will outlast castles and cathedrals. No one, I imagine, would have been more disbelieving than Offa himself if some flatterer of his court had foretold that his bank, his *clawdd* as the Welsh call it, would still be leaping high and strong across these uplands in 1,200 years' time and would still be helping, by its symbolism, to divide the two nations. After a further 1,200 years will the Dyke still be there? And still dividing?

Quiet uplands continue south from Kerry Hill all along the border to Radnor Forest and beyond to the Wye. They also cross the Wye south-west to climb sharply to the wide moorland called Epynt where quietness ends, for Epynt is a military range. But militarism, let us hope, will not last for ever and will someday be gone even from Epynt; and then the slopes will once more dip away down to the Usk in peace. Beyond Usk you are faced with stronger country—the challenging scarps of Brecon Beacons and Black Mountains—all good, lofty places that have their quintessential charm. But if I had to select just one upland to take my visitors to, I would choose, I think, the Black Mountains which are the remains of an ancient plateau long since sliced up by deep and narrow valleys into a range of grassy, rounded summits. We would tackle that exhilarating high-level walk from Hay Bluff in the north to Pen Cerrig-calch away in the south, climbing to some splendid hills in between and looking, all day, across an enormous sweep of wilder Wales and its borders. Next day, for a contrast, we would wander through the valleys. At Capel-y-ffin we would pay our respects to the ancient yews that guard the burial-ground there, for no British trees are more venerable than yews. Then downstream to the ruins of Llanthony Priory of which just enough survives to illustrate the high craftsmanship in stonework of the twelfth and thirteenth centuries. From there we would find a way round the lanes to the secretive little church of Partrishow, so remote in place and time, a quite remarkable medieval fragment that survives among hidden dingles as if the modern world had never happened. Its carved screen and rood loft speak of ancient oaks and ancient skills and a life so very different from our own.

So to the far south and to Gwent. I would like to introduce my friends to Gwent in the most Romantic way, with the aid of water and moonlight. Put them into a boat at Chepstow some warm summer's night and take them up the Wye on a flooding spring tide under a full moon. For if they had read anything at all about the history of English travel they would know that already by the end of the eighteenth century the Wye tour, complete with moonlight river excursions, was obligatory among the devotees of the new cult of the Picturesque. We know how seriously some of them took it, this Picturesque, writing long dissertations like those of William Gilpin and Sir Uvedale Price, dissecting the scenery detail by detail and criticizing it mercilessly if it failed to come up to their ideas of what constituted a well-composed landscape. Gilpin even admits somewhere that, had he dared, he would have taken a hammer to certain parts of Tintern Abbey because they 'are not only disagreeable in themselves, but confound the perspective'.

The proclaiming of the beauties of the Wye by the pioneer Romantics brought its inevitable result. A host of lesser writers descended on the valley, chiefly guide-book authors and landscape lyricists who found themselves so awe-struck at every ivied ruin, beetling crag and billowing woodland between Ross and Chepstow that you could be forgiven for wondering whether they really came to admire the curving Wye so much as the extravagancies of their own emotions. Yet though they overdid the paeons and the rhapsodies, they helped to set a trend that we still follow. They in their day came slowly down the valley in carriages, on horse, on foot or in boats, in discreet little parties or poetically alone. And we speed down in coaches and cars, in multitudes. They called the area picturesque, sublime, astonishing, majestic, stupendous. And we, rising as near to ecstasy as planners' English will go, call it an Area of Outstanding Natural Beauty which we hastily cut down to A.O.N.B. By which we mean, I trust, a place that we are resolved to treat with the utmost respect and where developers and speculators will always be told very firmly that they can take their philistine schemes elsewhere. Too naïve a hope? My companions might well ask: in a land like Britain, with urban millions exploding into the countryside nearly every weekend, isn't it likely that by christening a place an A.O.N.B. (or maybe a National Park) we draw unnecessary attention to it and so give it the kiss of death?

Where better to look for an answer to this question than farther west, in Gower, for instance, or on the Pembroke coast, where holiday-trade and second-home pressures are enormous? Gower is an A.O.N.B. with Swansea literally breathing down its neck when east winds blow. And, being a peninsula, it is also a cul-de-sac where traffic problems are acute and where at the end of a summer's day more touring caravans may arrive than there is space for. So to enjoy the best of Gower today you need to travel it on foot, as far away from the roads as possible. You need to take to the cliff-paths that still go gaily westward from Caswell Bay and lift you high above the waves, among sea-birds, cliff-edge flowers and winds off the ocean. So you go on, light-footed and light-hearted along the springing turf by way of Pennard and its fragmented castle, Threecliff Bay and Oxwich which has, despite its popular beach and vast car-park, a very fine, bird-rich reed-swamp that is a National Nature Reserve. West of Oxwich, and especially west of Port Eynon, where the main road abruptly dies, the coast gets even wilder, even more botanically interesting (with several rare limestone species protected in clifftop reserves). The breeze gets ever stronger, the rock beds more broken and tilted above secretive little coves. Then after the long thin finger of Worms Head (which the Welsh call Pen Pyrod) the coast turns you north and you look along the simple, incomparable curve of Rhosili Bay where summer waves curl softly but where winter storms come screaming in from far out in the Atlantic. Which no doubt explains why the Neolithic tombs perched above the little cliffs have long ago sloughed their great capstones. How refreshing it is to look along the whole three miles of this perfect bay and see no shack or caravan anywhere on its slopes nor breaking into skylines. It is important that this rare primal wildness shall continue. And that all the other unspoilt fragments of Gower shall remain inviolate. For like so much that is beautiful, this is very fragile, very vulnerable country.

To show my friends the best of the Pembroke Coast National Park would not be easy, there is so much that is best. Though of course all is not perfect along the 160 miles of coastal path there are very many places where they would find themselves in a splendour of shoreline scenery. And as they moved west along the southern coast they would see how the land has defied the ocean in one place and given way in another, so forming a marvellous succession of headlands and inlets, the promontories getting ever finer all the way to Stackpole Head which drops sheer and has great seas pouring through it, for it is hollowed beneath. From Stackpole Head you look to the even wilder cape called St. Govans. And once there you turn to face the real winds as you follow the limestone cliffs, with their crags, stacks, clefts and blow-holes and their lovely flowers and birds, all the seven or eight miles to Linney Head. Wales has nothing to show more fair if the day is shining, green seas are rolling and white water is breaking below you.

At Milford Haven we would take a boat and go out round St. Ann's Head, praying for a halcyon day. For only then can a small craft go round the island of Grassholm which stands far into the loneliness of the sea and six days in every seven belongs to the winds and the spume. The gannets of Grassholm, the thousands of gleaming white gannets are the greatest bird-spectacle in Wales. And on Grassholm, though it is a bird sanctuary, they are protected much more by wind and wave than by the guardianship of man. What threatens them is what threatens all sea-birds, all sea-life, and ultimately all other life. I mean the pollution of the oceans by oil, by the depositing of industrial wastes, by the poisons brought down by rivers, by sewage from coastal towns.

From Grassholm we would go to Skomer and circle it in our boat, for that is the best way to get the feel of any island that belongs essentially to the birds. There we would see but not disturb the dove-like kittiwakes sitting in neat rows on their seaweed nests rank above rank all the way up the cliffs. Puffins would whirr past or sit scattered upon the water. Then away we would go up the coast of St. Bride's Bay past multicoloured cliffs of tilted, arched and faulted beds of rock that speak of the immense timespan that went into the breaking down and rebuilding of earth's materials from the Pre-Cambrian to the Carboniferous.

Then to Ramsey Sound where I hope a spring tide would be flooding and roaring northwards through the Bitches, the row of dangerous fangs that stretch out from the island towards the mainland. Through the Bitches we would slip as between the cutwaters of a bridge and be swept on up the channel to turn east round the mainland point to land gently on the beach at White-sands Bay, the way sea-venturing people have reached St. Davids down all the centuries. I would want my friends to see St. Davids. But not only because of its charmingly unpretentious cathedral set modestly in a hollow and built with delicately purple rocks cut from the near-by sea-cliffs. No, there is more to St. Davids than the cathedral. There is the feel of the whole district, the strong sense that here is a corner of Wales which not only has special links with the past but, placed out there in a land of wild cliffs and singing winds, is palpably apart from the rest of Wales, the rest of Britain. The landscape is unmistakably ancient—those igneous outcrops towering along the northern sky, the stark rocks going out to the headland, the traces here and there of prehistoric man. And for more recent human history, the Middle Ages so strongly about you—the cathedral itself; the skeletal but endearing ruins of the Bishops' Palace; the shoreline chapels where pilgrims gave thanks for safe arrivals; and the shadowy line called Ffos y Mynach (Monk's Dyke) a simple bank of earth, still fragmentarily surviving, and which, maybe as far back as the Dark Ages, marked off this tip of western Wales as a private domain.

So we might go on along this inviting coast, out round the headlands of Strumble and Dinas that look north over the sea towards Bardsey; then round the bay of Newport to Cemaes and the Park's end. It is still so sound, so good, so uninjured, nearly all of it, that you tremble as you enjoy it. The old uneasy question nags at the back of your mind: is it in the end good for a region to make it a National Park in the British as distinct from the Swiss interpretation of the term? Is this not a cue for the developers to regard the place as a Klondyke? Few people have a sharper eye on such matters than John Barrett who lives on the shore with the coastal path outside his garden gate and who has long been involved with the Park and battled valiantly for its conservation. In a *Newsletter* of the Council for the Protection of Rural Wales he described how in one year: 'The National Park Committee had to deal with more than a thousand applications for planning permission to develop within the Park. Overwhelmingly these

concern holiday accommodation and second homes. Inevitably the
rate accelerates at which the splendour of our coast is diminished.
Just because he owns land on the coast a man has no predestined
right to profit from tourist development.' What attracts the great
majority of people to the Pembroke Coast National Park is the
surviving stretches of unmarred beauty. But development has
been so unbridled in the Tenby-Saundersfoot area that 'a visitor',
reports Barrett, 'finds unspoilt countryside only by leaving the
designated area. Just consider the irony, to find lovely country
you have to *leave* the Park.' So people go motoring along narrow,
twisting lanes in a desperate search for undeveloped beaches. As
the traffic grows year by year the threat increases that each little
valley down to the shore will find its access lane widened,
straightened and deprived of all its charm. There are known
answers to this problem (car parks well inland and frequent
minibuses going down to the shore) but the Park authorities
need to have a firm resolve to apply them. In addition to the
holiday industry the Pembroke Coast National Park is also afflicted
by the sight of oil refineries which are a lamentable disfigurement
of the shores of Milford Haven and which, given the successful
exploitation of Celtic Sea oil, could develop into something far
more devastating. As long as Gross National Product remains
our only god, one wonders what hope there is for the survival of
any of our national parks?

I would not need to tell any Americans in my party about the
troubles of national parks. They have Yosemite, Yellowstone and
others with their awe-inspiring litter problems, their frantic
traffic congestion and their impressive crime rate. Are our British
parks doomed to go the same way? Or shall we be able to teach
people how to use the parks, respect them, understand them
before it is too late and these cherished areas are devastated? The
faith is that we can. And you can see this faith in action if you take
yourself up to the moorland called Mynydd Illtud in the Brecon
Beacons National Park. There, at the admirable Mountain Centre
built for the purpose, you will find the Park fully explained with
the aid of photographs and literature—its geology, topography,
natural and human history. And from there you can set out to

explore the hills and valleys of the Park from the Black Mountains
in the east to the confusingly named Black Mountain in the west.
Or you simply sit and drink tea and look quietly out of the window
at the ancient sandstone hills.

In 1972 a new park in south-central Wales was designated (it
has not yet come into being)—the Cambrian Mountains National
Park, a delightful region that climbs up and over the hills between
the Dyfi and the Tywi; forty miles of sparsely peopled uplands
and valleys for which, strangely enough, no man in all the centuries has invented a name that has endured. 'Ellennith' is what
Giraldus calls it from the shadows of the twelfth century. But if
the name was ever current it soon died out and though in modern
times people have tried to revive it they have met with scant
success. And maybe 'Ellennith' was not a good name after all, not
good Welsh I mean. For in 1908 an editor of Giraldus's work
corrected it to 'Melenydd or Maelienydd'.

Call it what you will, this Ellennith is a part of Wales I would
much want my friends to see. We would enter it from the north (it
has no more delightful approach) by following some tributary of
the Dyfi back to its source. Choose Leri, Clettwr, Einion, Llyfnant
—it hardly matters which because all come down through attractively broken country gnawed by dark gorges where waters splash
cold and are overhung by crooked little oaks some of whose
boughs are green even in winter from the ferns that hang along
them. Whichever valley we climbed we would come up at last to
Plynlimon, a name that is an Anglicization of the Welsh Pum-
lumon, which apparently means the Five Beacons. And lurking in
the background is another name, long forgotten, that was evidently given, like Ellennith, not to Plynlimon alone but to the
whole of these uplands. The name is Moruge; and it, too, comes
from Giraldus. In 1188 he journeys north from Strata Florida
towards Llanbadarn Fawr 'having on our right the lofty mountains
of Moruge which in Welsh are called Ellennith'. I wonder what
happened to 'Moruge' that it died out so completely? Not that
we can really regret the loss of a name not only so English but also
so joyless, the sort of name Tolkien might have used for some
disquieting place his hobbits had to pass through on their way to

Mordor. 'Moruge', says Giraldus, contains the idea of 'moors and bogs'—a fitting name for this high reach of country where spongy tracts are everywhere.

Plynlimon itself is certainly one of the great viewpoints. From up there, some clean-washed day between depressions, I would show my companions more of both north and south Wales than can be seen from anywhere. And I would wish them to follow the ridge from end to end, preferably from south to north to keep the light behind us all the way. We would walk the short mountain turf and feel lichens and clubmosses crisp underfoot. We would see high-placed cairns that have survived 3,000 years since the Bronze Age. I could point to the major intrusions that our century has contributed to the scene: the thousands of acres of conifers on the east, the hydroelectric reservoir on the west and leave my visitors to judge them. They would see, too, the decaying relics of the last 200 years—the crumpled ruins of lead-mines, the shattered upland houses, the shadowy outlines of cottages whose stones have quite gone, cottages in which lived poverty-cursed Welsh smallholders who had little option except to try their luck at farming these worthless, rush-infested moorlands after the rich had helped themselves to so many of the better valley lands by acts of enclosure.

Of Plynlimon's streams it is the Severn (or Hafren) that will contribute least to this proposed Park unless somebody shaves a broad swathe of conifers off the first few miles of its banks. For as things are, the poor Hafren is lost in the spruce blanket and by the time it escapes from the darkness, it is out of the Park and gone. The Wye does better. The Wye gets through the conifer zone fairly quickly and for many a coloured mile past Llangurig and Rhayader to Newbridge it marks the eastern frontier of the region. The third stream, the once unfettered little Rheidol, now suffers the indignity of being divided into two, one part being poured down a pipe to work a turbine. Which means that for its finest few miles, its deep gorge from Ponterwyd to Devil's Bridge, it has lost its old cutting power. But we can be thankful that before man got his hands on it the Rheidol enjoyed a few million years shaping great scenery for us out of the Silurian shales; and will do so again when the hydroelectric scheme has had its day.

The place to enjoy the Rheidol at its best is Parson's Bridge. There is so much to see, so much to learn, by simply walking down that steep woodland path to the bottom of the gorge. There you meet with forest which may well be primeval: for not even the most rapacious have deemed it worth risking their necks to get at these crooked, stunted oaks and birches. So, quite rightly, it has become a National Nature Reserve, this dark, cool gorge with its ancient, mossy trees, its many summer pied fly-catchers, its wildflowers (there is an unexpected stripe of lime-stone that bears calcicole plants such as rock stonecrop and marjoram), its mosses and its ferns, and its deeply pot-holed riverbed far down between the rocks.

Not many flaps of a buzzard's wing southwards you come to Devil's Bridge. In the eighteenth century I'm sure Devil's Bridge was perfection—a place where gorges met in the forest depths and there was hardly a sign of man except for the trackway that scrambled down to the ancient bridge across the Mynach stream and up the other side. Today it is all commercialized; and what should be a place of beauty to uplift your spirit meets you instead with a turnstile and a picture-postcard stall. But let us not wholly despair. Some day a generation with a surer sense of values than ours will feel moved to do away with these abominations.

Mercifully the upper Ystwyth, Rheidol's sister stream a few miles south, is not yet so exploited for tourism (though surely the caravans on the site of Hafod Uchdryd mansion ought to be moved to a less conspicuous, less historic spot?). Here I would tell my companions about the builder of Hafod, Thomas Johnes, who created a characteristic eighteenth-century Arcadia-style estate in this then remote vale. And I would recommend them to read *Peacocks in Paradise* by Elizabeth Inglis-Jones who relates the saga so well. What Johnes found in the Ystwyth was a valley long bereft of its forests by the lead-smelters. What he left behind were slopes set with millions of oaks, beeches and larches, trees that are now nearly all gone but of which a few groves survive as a memorial to their enthusiastic planter. The rest of Hafod's

L

slopes are now mostly covered by conifers of the Forestry Commission.

The lead-zinc-silver-mine at Cwmystwyth, spreading far and conspicuous along the right bank of the river, is admittedly squalid. Yet, far more than Hafod, this is a place of history and as such deserves our respect. So I trust that some means will be found of getting rid of its blemishes while retaining its more interesting features—the evidences of mining going back perhaps to prehistory. Though Cwmystwyth mine's heyday falls into modern times, for me it is especially a link with Strata Florida Abbey and the Middle Ages, a period that so often seems to come close to us in that part of Wales, not only because the Cistercians were very busy thereabouts for so long a time but because the activities that preoccupied them—sheep farming and lead mining —are activities that have gone on shaping the scene right into our own century.

It was a quirk of the Cistercians to give some of their abbeys fancy Latin names. So they had Alba Landa near Whitland, Strata Marcella near Welshpool. And near Tregaron, isolated between the hills and the great bog, they founded Strata Florida whose probably splendid buildings are now all gone except for what lies fragmented on the ground and for one remaining admirable Norman arch which neither time, weather nor vandals have been able to destroy. Medieval place-names, too, have proved remarkably durable in these parts. You come down the road from the abbey to cross the Teifi at Pontrhydfendigaid (Bridge by the Blessed Ford). You turn north and are soon at the site of a medieval *ysbyty* or hospice called Ysbyty Ystwyth. You cross the Ystwyth at Pontrhydygroes (Bridge by the Ford of the Cross) and soon you are passing over the gorge at the Devil's Bridge which in Welsh retains its medieval name, Pont ar Fynach (Monk's Bridge). Another *ysbyty* awaits you just up the road, Ysbyty Cynfyn (Hospice of St. Cynfyn) and here is a little country church within what is left of a prehistoric stone circle. (Can we assume that this has been uninterruptedly a centre of religion, first pagan then Christian, for maybe three thousand years?) The road goes on north then east to the top of Plynlimon Pass where again the

Middle Ages has bequeathed us a place-name: Eisteddfa Gurig (Seat of St. Curig) so called, we may assume, because Curig, an itinerant Dark Ages missionary, stayed here and preached when on his way to found his church at Llangurig, an event the Middle Ages no doubt commemorated by setting up a wayside shrine at the top of the pass.

The narrow track that used to wind over the moorlands by way of Eisteddfa Gurig eventually became our main road of today. But a similar high-level, medieval route parallel to it is now nearly lost and forgotten. This was the Cistercians' way, the track that took them from Strata Florida up and over their sheepwalks past the glinting, watershed lakes called Teifi Pools. The country up there is all a beautiful, far-seeing, lark-singing grassland which I pray will never be planted up with the dreaded spruces such as have virtually obliterated Llyn Berwyn, a lake to the south, and many a once open slope between Strata Florida and the upper Tywi.

Leading my party by Teifi Pools I would continue over the sweet-smelling hills along the monks' ancient way to where it crosses the Elan. (Not that we shall be able to do this much longer: if present reservoir proposals are accepted the upper Elan will be drowned, thus cutting the line of the old road.) Beyond the Elan the track climbs and drops again, this time to the Wye near where the Marteg stream flows in. But no pause yet. On climbs the path to yet a further ridge against the sky before it comes down its final slope into the long, green valley of Cwmhir where the Cistercians raised but never quite completed what, John Leland tells us, was the greatest church in all Wales. Go and measure it for yourself—the stumps of its walls are there yet.

South from this pathway of the Middle Ages the moorland undulates in beauty through a world of rock and grass till it plunges at last to the gorges and side-dingles of the Tywi and its tributaries. This valley of the higher Tywi will ever remind me of one day (I am astonished to think it will soon be thirty years ago) when I crossed these hills on my bicycle. I had ridden through wintry weather all the thirty-five or so hard miles from Ponterwyd (where Penny and I were then living in a tiny cottage called

Bwlch Gwair). I came by way of Tregaron and the long climb up Cwm Berwyn to cross the moors on a track that had not yet been polluted by tarmacadam and which forded one stream after another where now there are motorable bridges. Then down the rough twisting road that followed the Tywi and so at last to Rhandirmwyn, highest village on the river. Here I called on Captain and Mrs. Vaughan who were living, farming, gardening, growing apples and keeping bees at a house of much charm called Nantymwyn. With the Vaughans I discussed what might be done to protect the red kite, the magnificent bird of prey once widespread in Britain but by the 1940s reduced to a sorry remnant miraculously surviving in south-central Wales. A result of this and similar meetings with other people was the formation of the Kite Committee, a group of enthusiasts who over the years since then have anxiously watched the Welsh kite population increase very slowly from about ten pairs to its present figure of nearly thirty.

Today the Kite Committee, which is now a joint committee of the R.S.P.B. and the Nature Conservancy Council, still includes several of the original team, notably Colonel Morrey Salmon of Cardiff, a man who knows more than anyone about the history of kites and kite protection, for in his long life he has seen so much of it at first hand. The Vaughans, too, have gone on battling ever since in the cause of conservation not only of kites but of all Welsh wildlife, both animals and plants, and of Welsh people too, the country people and the beautiful but threatened world in which they live.

I think it can be said of the Vaughans that for them the kite has become, over the years, a symbol, as well as a rare bird in need of protection—a symbol standing for everything in the life of rural Wales that is good and precious and worth struggling for in the face of the many forms of despoliation that always threaten. I suspect, too, that an encouraging number of other people are beginning to feel the same, not only naturalists and conservationists, but also Welsh hill-farmers and country folk. Many of them today, when they observe a kite circling over the sheepwalks, see something more than a bird; they see something especially Welsh and therefore something especially to be safeguarded.

A few miles upstream of Rhandirmwyn the deep, winding gorge of the Tywi is now drowned by a long narrow reservoir. So another wilderness was destroyed. Not only by the reservoir but also by its access roads that have become tourist routes and have caused a pestilence of cars and coaches to intrude upon a hitherto tranquil region, bringing noise, fumes, traffic jams, crowds—urban horrors that have no proper place in the hill country. In the same way in the 1960s another totally quiet upland was ripped open to admit the tourist throngs by the creation of Nanty-y-moch reservoir under Plynlimon. Likewise the solitudes of the Elan valley were invaded late last century by the Birmingham waterworks.

It is often said that nobody uses their legs these days, that everybody motors. But this is not true. There are many people walking the hills of Wales at all seasons, and increasingly so, and what they feel is that they have a right to walk them as near-wilderness areas not as regions criss-crossed by motor roads. After all, in a country as small as Wales, a motorist can get his vehicle to practically everywhere. So I make this plea: that when the next round of Welsh reservoirs comes along, the tourist routes be left out of the scheme. Because if they are not we shall end with our mountains and moorlands being completely net-worked by roads and then there will be no escaping the car anywhere at all.

Though the Tywi gorge has gone, there are exquisite neighbouring valleys that survive (but for how much longer?). They are valleys that owe much of their charm to the sizeable oakwoods that climb up long, steep slopes to often craggy skylines. In the cwm called Gwenffrwd the R.S.P.B. owns a reserve of surpassing beauty: it has fine sheepwalks, oakwoods and moorlands and is the habitat of a wide range of animals, birds and plants. And its acquisition by the R.S.P.B. was a result of the Vaughans' work for conservation, for it was they who first suggested it.

Having shown my visitors the many splendours of Gwenffrwd we could then take the lane that slips over the watershed and down the valley of the Cothi with its crags and steep-tilted oakwoods. And so into the west, going right across country till we reached yet another choice region of Wales—the coast of Ceredigion. I am aware of the blemishes on this coastline and of the threat of perhaps worse to come. Yet despite the caravans that fill the view here and there, despite a big military establishment defiling one of the best headlands, there is still a lot that conservationists are fighting to save from the sort of ribbon development that has this century down-graded so much of the south coast of England. Two lengths of the Ceredigion shore I value especially: the cliffs that go south from Aberystwyth for about ten magnificent miles; and the delightful hills, glens and sea crags between New Quay and Aberporth. These long stretches of cliffland, flowery slopes and pebbly shore have kept a great deal of their wildness. There are miles of yellow gorse and heather, and elegant, tall grasses; and even woods of ancient cliff-edge oaks, kept dwarf by salty tempests off the sea. Buzzards, ravens, choughs and sea-birds nest in safety along the precipices. Seals lie out on flat wet rocks, asleep and undisturbed. And everywhere there is the beauty of shape and colour that comes with time and rain, frost and sun and sea winds.

Then, at the northern tip of Ceredigion's coast, we would come to the dunes of Ynys-las which, like other dunes farther north at Mochras, Harlech and Newborough, are full of flowers and butterflies and are a National Nature Reserve. But how many equally fine or finer dunes round the coast of Wales are unprotected in any way? Everywhere there is need of special safeguards for dune areas: all are threatened, or soon must be, as the demand for land increases.

So with estuaries. They, too, are open spaces, comparatively unused and therefore frighteningly vulnerable. They can be reclaimed as farmlands, dammed to make reservoirs, harnessed for electricity. Or they can be built on, turned into airports or barraged to make coastal roads. Some in time undoubtedly will be so destroyed. But never, I pray, so fair an estuary as the Dyfi. I mentioned in Chapter 1 that last century a large scheme of reclamation was planned for this estuary. And that only a few years ago there was a proposal to barrage it. It is inevitable that some new project will threaten sooner or later. But when it does I

hope its promoters will take themselves some bright day to the
mouth of the river and go out across the sands to where they can
see east up the estuary. Let them take a long and honest look at
that fair scene which has remained unchanged except in a few
details for thousands of years: all those surrounding hills of
Meirionnydd, Montgomery and Ceredigion; the shining wet sands
in the foreground, the winding creeks, the ever-moving tides.
And let them ask themselves if it is truly so desperately necessary
that this perfect little estuary should be dammed or barraged or
reclaimed or interfered with in any way at all. Let them resolve
the matter there and then, out in the wind and the sunshine. (Too
many such decisions are made within walls and under roofs.) And
let them not forget that this estuary is a National Nature Reserve
that extends from the Dyfi bar for six miles upriver to where it
neighbours Ynys-hir. And that the Dyfi estuary and Ynys-hir
together form the chief haunt of wildfowl and waders in central
Wales. Conservationists must be ready to do battle for this little
estuary should it ever be threatened. And not only the estuary: the
whole delectable Dyfi valley should be declared a conservation
area now, before it is too late.

⚘ 10. Gardening for the Birds

When Penny and I went to stay with our botanist friend Mary Richards in Zambia we found her living in a house with a beautiful garden surrounded by endless miles of wild bush. It was an exciting stretch of country varied by hills, marshes and different types of woodland. But in our walks through those dry woods with their sandy soils and frequent rocky outcrops, we invariably found fewer birds and butterflies than in Mary Richards's garden —a well-watered clearing with lawns, flower-beds, scented shrubs and a great variety of trees, some natural, some foreign. This superiority of gardens as a refuge for wildlife, especially woodland creatures, is not something peculiar to Africa. It is, I'm sure, the same all over the world. Why? Because in a garden of the right sort insects, birds and small animals find more food, water, shelter and peace than in many a wild habitat.

Gardeners are often creators of oases in an unkind world. Certainly when we came to make our garden at Ynys Edwin it was shelter we had to establish before anything else, shelter at the side of an estuary that is a fly-way for frigid easterlies racing down off the Cambrian mountains in winter and for salt-laden gales which can blow up off the Atlantic at any time of the year. Our only advantage was the *ynys* itself: its rocks and wind-shaped oaks protect us a little from the north. The rest of our world was a bleak desert of bog and rough pasture trampled and chewed by numerous cattle and ponies and nibbled incessantly by sheep.

We began one February day by making a fence to keep out the stock. Inside that we put a hedge. Then we lovingly planted shrub after shrub, making sure that their roots were all cosseted round with compost and sand. Not that we had to wait many months before our garden showed signs of becoming more birdful than the surrounding fields. By late April the simple act of fencing and

168

letting the grass grow brought us a pair of tree pipits. We rejoiced in the male bird's cheering voice as he sang among the young yellow oak leaves. From up there, too, a willow warbler let his delicate phrases fall gently into the garden and a pair of these most sweet-voiced of all warblers have nested with us every spring since.

Quicker than we had dared to hope the hedges grew—cypress, lonicera, hawthorn, berberis, briar rose and box. The shrubs bushed out and ever so little the winds were rebuffed, giving the garden a climate of its own. Where its lower edge merges into the peat bog Penny planted the purple-twigged willow, *Salix daphnoides*, which soon grew tall and bore bright yellow catkins into which redpolls buried their crimson foreheads in search, I suppose, of nectar. Birches we did not need to plant. Their seedlings sprang spontaneously in our damp acid soil and were soon as lofty as the willows and providing ample seed for autumn finches.

For ground cover we began by sowing *Limnanthes douglasii* and this we have never had cause to regret. It has spread into great patches on our wet soil (which would otherwise be infested with common rush and water blinks) and its yellow and white flowers are marvellously attractive to bees. For bushier ground cover we put in alpine rhododendrons, heathers, berberis, vacciniums and azaleas—all good sites for the robins' nests we never find till we come along transplanting and mulching in autumn. A biennial that has scattered itself generously is forget-me-not. On its seeds the midsummer linnets, young and old, feed eagerly day after day; and one memorable spring a pair of willow warblers placed their domed nest in the heart of this blue forget-me-not carpet. (It was the most beautifully sited nest I had seen since many years ago I found a blackbird's nest right on the ground amongst the bluebells in a wood in Worcestershire.) For shelter and fragrance at the western end of the garden we put tree heaths and escallonias that now make a thicket where thrushes and wrens love to nest.

In time our garden began to resemble the most bird-rich type of natural woodland with a canopy of high branches arching over a thick and varied shrub layer and a wealth of flowering plants and ferns. But not too dense a woodland. The best woods for birds have clearings and glades to provide freedom of movement and variety of feeding and breeding places. A woodland margin is also attractive to birds, so many of which like to be able to fly out and forage in the fields. So a garden that has tall trees, especially oaks, in the background and shrubs and herbage of different sizes and species in the foreground, as well as spaces provided by paths and lawns, such a garden meets the needs of many woodland birds.

It was an invaluable start for our garden to have the old oaks alongside, for no tree is more infested with edible and nutritious caterpillars—oak rollers, winter moths, mottled umbers and many others—just when the woodland birds need unlimited supplies to feed their young on. Long and narrow, its upper side the oak-clad hill, its lower side the peat bog, our garden became a slice of woodland edge and we rejoiced each year to see more and more birds making use of it. As everything grew, a natural ladder developed linking ground to shrub, shrub to birch and willow and from there to the oak boughs. So all through spring and summer there were birds feeding, courting or nesting at every height of the vegetation. Walls were another dimension we could not waste. On the front of the house we nailed pig-wire from ground to eaves and up it climbed roses, jasmine, clematis and a trumpet vine, all bringing food and shelter for birds and insects.

There is nothing like a thick hedge for birds' nests; and blackbirds, song thrushes, hedge sparrows and chaffinches were soon building in ours. Missel-thrushes chose an ivied fork in an oak, then an old holly we had enclosed within the garden. But in a year or two they were nesting in the white, deliciously scented *Clematis montana wilsonii* on the wall of the house. It was five years before greenfinches bred in the garden—in a mixed hedge of sweet briar and hawthorn—and they filled our days with their laughing notes the summer through. One year we had goldfinch music as well. A flock of them are always with us in winter, for there are teazels and burdocks just outside the garden. But these lovely finches had always gone elsewhere to breed until one spring when they built their mossy little nest at the top of a lilac. Our first whitethroat's nest—in the heart of a potentilla—was also an occasion for rejoicing. But I think it was when the first garden warbler arrived with his rich and hastening song and immediately began to build wispy false nests in a hypericum, then a philadelphus and finally made a real nest in a gooseberry bush, that we felt that we really had achieved a bird garden. Since then we have had this splendid songster with us every year and sometimes two pairs have bred, the males challenging each other with their songs all through May.

This past spring a pair of long-tailed tits have nested in a cypress close to the house. What more endearing birds could we have—so delicately coloured, so unobtrusive, so confiding. They went to and fro in the garden all day long, keeping in touch with each other by the faintest of chirrups and 'stic-stic' notes, never getting excited at our presence, scarcely aware, it seemed that we existed. Often they flew only inches above Penny's head as she bent over her plants. They have another virtue that makes them good value as a garden bird: they took weeks and weeks to build their wonderful bottle of a nest. Back and forth from garden wall to cypress they flew with bits of lichen and moss that were sometimes so tiny we couldn't see them without binoculars. It was such a slow process that a pair of neighbouring robins built, laid, incubated, reared their young and departed while the long-tailed tits were still building. For the whole of the spring they became a part of our lives, these tits, until the day they brought out their numerous family. An hour later all had gone across the marsh to the woods, and we did not see long-tailed tits in the garden again till autumn when, united with other tits in an excited, sharp-voiced bird party, they came many times to search our willows, oaks and birches for tiny insects.

Gardeners speak of hungry soils. But there are hungry houses too. Any house put together as crudely as Ynys Edwin was about three centuries ago, its walls made of poor local shale and built two or three feet thick with a filling of loose rubble, any such house is certain to be a hungry house. No matter how generous you are with fertilizer a hungry soil will always ask for more. So with some old houses: you are always feeding them—repairing walls, mending the roof, trying to stop the chimney from smoking or damp from rising or your feet from freezing on slate floors. Over the years we have filled in many a hole in the walls of Ynys Edwin, which is good for the house but it deprived certain birds of their breeding places. Fortunately they were all birds who are just as happy to be accommodated in nest boxes attached to trees or walls.

So every year we have five hole-nesting birds in boxes in or just outside the garden: blue tit, great tit, spotted flycatcher, pied flycatcher and redstart. And, except for the self-effacing spotted flycatcher, what a quarrelsome lot they are! For about a week at the height of the box-choosing season there is endless bickering and chivvying as a pied flycatcher, with a flurry of black and white feathers, swoops to drive off a tit. Or he in turn is shooed away by a fury of red, white, blue and black as a cock redstart comes at him like a hawk. We are glad when it's all sorted out and each pair is more or less quietly building. Then comes the idyllic moment of the year—every May without fail—just a few still, sunny days when the garden is full of redstart and pied flycatcher song from dawn to dusk.

Usually the first pied flycatcher arrives in our garden in the third week of April. Clearly his repeated two or three notes— 'Too-swee-too-swee-too-switty-swee'—come to us with the scent of magnolias through the open bedroom window. And for a while our life is different. For their nest-box is on our window-ledge and nothing must be allowed to disturb them in those first few days when they are settling in. So we creep about, indoors and out, feeling like trespassers. When that delicate stage is over we return to normal because once pied flycatchers are established they become very bold, the male especially. From the moment of his arrival he comes to the box without hesitation. Though fresh from Africa he is instantly more familiar with us than most of the birds we have been feeding in the garden all winter. He spends hours singing on the box and popping in and out of it—this being his way of demonstrating to rivals, be they tits, redstarts or fly-catchers, that this is his box. In three or four days along comes a hen pied flycatcher and in no time she is carrying dead leaves and old grass stems into the box and making a very neat little cup for her seven or eight green-blue eggs. By this date we are often eat-out of doors, just a few feet below the nest. But the flycatchers ignore us. The male stands on the box singing on and on, while the female hides inside it incubating her eggs.

Some years redstarts have nested in a box ten feet from the fly-catchers on another bedroom sill. But how differently they behave. A redstart would not sing on his box with us at our garden table below. He will certainly be singing, for he never seems to stop all day, but it will be from the highest twig of an oak above the garden or behind the house. To me there is a particular quality of wild-ness in the redstart's song, especially in his tremulous opening phrase. What follows varies from bird to bird: it may be a rattle, a hoarse squeak or sometimes a long plaintive sentence of indefin-able beauty. Of all spring's delights one of the sharpest is to hear the dawn song of redstarts answering each other through the near darkness, for they are usually the earliest birds to sing in our garden. Then the robins join in and these two species often have the still May dawn to themselves for half an hour before the first thrush shatters the morning and wakes the rest of nature.

Boldness and shyness are curiously merged in the redstart. Seeing a pair nesting in a box on our bedroom window-ledge, visitors have sometimes concluded that redstarts are as tame as robins. Far from it. They nest in our box because there are few other holes available. They remain very nervous, slipping fur-tively in and out, never staying to be looked at if they think any-one is about. Only early in the morning does the cock come to sing in the apple tree close to our window. Then, at four yards' range, his song is lovely to hear as it penetrates our waking dreams. And occasionally he comes to perch on the open window to look inquiringly into the bedroom. For a 'cave' like this is clearly something he feels he ought to explore. When they have a family to feed even the shyest birds can become very daring and for the last few days before the young leave the nest our window-ledge redstarts fly into the box with food regardless of our presence. They also become very noisy. All day we have to listen to their peevish 'too-ee-tic-tic' repeated so insistently we are quite glad to see the young leave the box one by one and then to hear the whole family gradually move away into the oaks, their anxious cries fading into the distance.

Whatever she plants, Penny has always given preference to the most scented species and varieties. So we have a fragrant garden. Which means a wealth of insects, some of which cheerfully eat our plants and sometimes us. But an insect-rich garden is sure to be a bird-rich garden and—let's keep a sense of proportion—only very few insects are a serious nuisance. The trouble is that gardeners for generations have been brainwashed by writers and advertisers into feeling compelled to rush for the poison-spray at the first sign of anything that flies or crawls. Some gardeners behave as if it is the end of the world if they find a few greenfly or a little black-spot on their roses. It is better to think twice before you bring out the lethal spray-gun: certainly you will kill the greenfly but you will also slaughter ladybirds, hoverflies, lacewings—all of which are devourers of greenfly. You will also rob your garden of a whole range of other lovely insects which are just as beautiful as many of your flowers. So we have always tried to be tolerant of what the world calls pests. Artificial though a garden is, we have wanted ours to be a home to as many wild species as reasonable. Rabbits and hares we have fenced out because as destroyers they are as bad as sheep and goats. In the kitchen garden we hand-pick caterpillars of the gooseberry sawfly and the large white butterfly because these the birds will not eat. But most pests we tolerate: otherwise if you get neurotic about every leaf that's nibbled you find yourself engaged in perpetual warfare. With traps, slug-death, insecticides and weed-killers you may achieve an immaculate garden: but it will be a very antiseptic sort of perfection. You often hear people asking where have all the butterflies gone? Yet the same people may be liberal users of insecticides in their gardens! In Ynys Edwin garden we have black-spot on some of our roses; slugs, snails, millipedes, woodlice, leather jackets and wire-worms are far from rare; the deadly bracket fungus may eventually kill one of our birches. We have no gun to shoot the bullfinches and our forsythias suffer as a result. But are not bullfinches at least as lovely as forsythia? Having no can of insecticide we have lots of greenfly; but if we had no greenfly on the roses, I doubt if we would have any long-tailed tits at all, for they take greenfly by the score. Our philosophy in the matter is simple: not willing to turn our garden into a battle-field we are prepared to accept a certain amount of damage with-out getting into rage or panic. We have given up trying to grow crocuses—too many are eaten by mice—but we have daffodils and hardy cyclamen instead.

Then all those articles, books and broadcasts about the perfect lawn. What a load of rubbish! But by persistent repetition they have achieved their effect so successfully that now there must be millions of suburban gardeners who would feel quite ashamed if someone spotted a plantain in their lawn. What does it matter if the grass is patched here and there by daisies or varied by lichens and mosses? (One of the loveliest lawns I ever saw was quite silvery with lichen but its owner never stopped apologizing about it.) If our little lawn at Ynys Edwin had no dandelions we would miss one of the most charming sights of the year—the moment when the young linnets are brought by their parents to be taught how to pick a dandelion clock to pieces.

Then there are the moles. What dread the sight of a molehill on the lawn engenders in gardeners! Yet is a molehill truly such a tragedy? Is it really necessary to set those nasty traps that squeeze a mole to death by slow torture? (Because a creature suffers underground out of your sight its death is no less agonizing.) Or do you prefer to put down worms baited with strychnine? Wouldn't it be better to accept the mole as a fascinating visitor worthy of study and admiration, an animal which merely wants to deprive your lawn of a few surplus worms and incidentally provide it with a sound drainage system? The chemical manufacturers will tell you how to rid your lawn of worms—there are some vilely noxious substances available for the purpose. But without worms what are the blackbirds and thrushes expected to live on? And as for moles: if a mole never stirred in our garden at Ynys Edwin then no buzzard would ever come to sit in the dead oak to watch for them in the early morning.

Though we have moles in the garden they are far outnumbered by wood mice and bank voles whose runs and burrows are everywhere. Which is not surprising because we never remove any leaf litter, fallen twigs and other debris of the autumn. Burning the dead leaves—there's another fetish of the tidy-minded! No wonder gardeners have to spend fortunes on fertilizers. Where do they think the natural fertility of the soil comes from? The leaf litter, if you examine it, you will find crawling with tiny animals all chewing away and helping the fungi and the bacteria to break the stuff down to form new soil that will sustain new life. Amongst it the little rodents find their sustenance. Then if they sometimes vary their diet and eat your tulip bulbs instead, the best thing is to give up growing tulips or grow them in mouse-proof boxes. After all, it isn't the fault of the voles and the mice if they are rather too plentiful. It is man who has destroyed many of their natural predators such as weasels and owls.

The wood mice we never see in our garden unless at night in the light of a torch we glimpse one leaping away into the darkness like a tiny kangaroo, his pure-white underside conspicuous for a moment. For wood mice are very nocturnal, as their big, bulging eyes suggest. It is different with bank voles—they have a certain entertainment value as we work in the garden because they are lively by day as well as by night and are always rustling about in piles of leaves or under rock plants. And sometimes we see them as they scuttle from one haven to another, their reddish backs easily identifying them. They love walls too. Six feet from the window of my writing room I look at a wall that has decorated itself with clumps of pennywort. And if I glance out of the window I occasionally see a bank vole reach out of a hole in the wall, nip off a succulent pennywort leaf and disappear into the wall with it. The whole exercise takes no more than a second because if you're as defenceless as a vole you don't expose yourself more than you need.

Having an abundance of mice, voles and shrews in the garden (and no dogs or cats) means that we also have owls, stoats and weasels. And that especially Welsh weasel, the polecat. This handsome, furry, black predator is mainly nocturnal but twice I have met with one in the garden in broad daylight, questing from side to side very methodically, nose to ground, evidently sniffing out small mammals. Each time the polecat passed me within a few feet but, as is often the way with woodland animals, it failed to see me standing quietly there.

Trying to be as tolerant as possible of what is usually called vermin we accept even the unpopular grey squirrels. They soon came down from the oaks to make quick, nervous forays into the garden. But it was not till the front of the house was thickly matted with climbers that they really settled down with us. Despite their bad reputation I don't think they do us much lasting damage. Certainly they are very sweet-toothed. We have seen them eating the creamy-white buds of our favourite climbing rose, Madame Alfred Carrière, and, more galling still, the red trumpets of campsis Madame Galen. Grey squirrels are said to be dreadful raiders of birds' nests yet I have never had reason to suspect they rob any of ours though they often pass close to several. If we were trying to grow specimen trees we would feel less genial towards grey squirrels but within the context of a garden nature reserve we feel able to suffer their occasional depredations in exchange for the delight of seeing them rippling so elegantly about the garden, leaping dramatically from tree to tree or sunbathing so ecstatically on our window-sills. Suppose, I sometimes ask myself, suppose they were red squirrels? Nobody stigmatizes red squirrels and calls them tree rats. Yet they used to do pretty nearly as much damage in the days when they were common. The red squirrel has gone, the grey has come. I would prefer the red but in its absence would rather have the grey than no squirrels at all. A woodland setting is not complete without squirrels of some sort.

From noxious animals to noxious plants. I have mentioned in an earlier chapter how we introduced giant hogweeds and how kind people warned us against them. It is certainly true what they said—these are formidable plants. Penny has had blisters come up on her arms simply from brushing past a giant hogweed on a hot day. But you can't destroy everything in nature that carries a sting or sharp teeth or poisonous fangs. And we do love our giant hogweed. We marvel at the speed with which it spreads its huge basal-leaves and shoots up its almost tree-like stem to maybe a dozen

M

feet, soon to crown it with a great head of creamy flowers. Then on these shapely umbels gather crowds of flies and beetles in pursuit of which come the birds, especially tits and warblers. All day they are there, weaving in and out of the umbel's intricate architecture, snapping up insects as they go. So in early August when in full bloom a giant hogweed is a natural bird-table. But you need to be at an upstairs window to get the best out of it.

If you don't fancy giant hogweeds or have no room for them, the ordinary common hogweed of waysides is just as good an insect attracter. Not that so mundane a plant is worth space in a garden. But you might have some odd corner just outside where it would love to be. Let it battle there with nettles, burdocks and thistles—all bad weeds it is true, but important to birds as well as insects. An annual weed that's a real treasure—but you will find it only on damp ground—is water-pepper. It certainly doesn't look much of a plant (a foot or so high with insignificant greenish-white flower spikes) but it is a prodigious seed-producer, keeping chaffinch flocks going all through winter. Bramblings, too, if you're lucky. It is one of Ynys Edwin's advantages that, being on ground that is marish (to revive an old word), we have generous beds of water-pepper just beyond the hedge where finches feed day after day.

There is a price to be paid for having so many birds in your garden: especially in the breeding season it becomes theirs as much as yours. They accept your presence but only with a great deal of grumbling. Go anywhere in the garden in May or June and you will be met with a bad-tempered 'churr' from a missel-thrush, the high, thin whine of a robin, a 'tut-tut-tut' from a blackbird, a splutter of curses from a wren. The garden warbler offers you an anxious 'check-check' as you enter his domain; the willow-warbler sounds genuinely hurt with his pathetic 'too-ee, too-ee'; the chaffinch's sharp-tongued 'twink-twink' leaves you in no doubt of what he thinks of you. And for quite unconcealed disgust there is the whitethroat who really does swear unmistakably. All this disapproval has its effect. You learn to tread softly through all these jealously claimed territories and you never dare stop anywhere long in case you're keeping somebody off their nest. It is almost enough to make us wish for the peace and silence of July. But no, we never wish the delicious days of spring away like that. Besides, July brings not only silence. It brings heat and thunderstorms and, worse than either, horseflies.

Some features of our garden are far from natural. The telephone wires, for instance, that we see from the kitchen window and the ugly poles that support them. But buzzards often perch on the poles and because these fine raptors are all differently marked we get to know them as individuals. There is the pale-headed one, the dark-breasted one and the one whose white tail makes him look just like a rough-legged buzzard. As for wires, we like them even less than poles, for wires are so dangerous to flying birds. Yet the simple truth is that the smaller birds adore them and we are always rushing to the window with binoculars to identify some newcomer perched up there so clear and easy to see. For birds a wire is a meeting place, a singing perch or a good position from which to look out for danger, food or fellow birds. Our best wire of all is a short length of clothes line just outside the window. In spring we can stand at the kitchen sink and have entrancing views of redstarts, both spotted and pied flycatchers and swallows at six-feet range.

Swallows! I could fill the rest of this book about the swallows of Ynys Edwin, they are so much a part of our lives from April till September. More so a few years ago, when we had six or seven pairs nesting, than now when they have dwindled to a pair or two only. It would be a great sadness if we lost them altogether, for no birds give us more delight than swallows as they come twittering through the garden snapping at insects just above our heads. That's on dull, windy days when the flies are forced low. When the depression has passed the swallows become more remote: but all day we hear them, or half hear them, as they enjoy the upper breezes; and we have only to look up to see them slipping easily along the sky, diving, climbing, circling, jerking to this side or that and always sounding full of excitement about everything they do.

Usually they nest in the adjacent farm buildings. But we have had a pair totally without fear of human kind. One spring, for instance, if we left the kitchen door open a male swallow often came swooping in, fluttered round and out again, giving us a wonderful blue gleam as his wings took the sunlight. Then when he found a mate they went round to the front of the house and began diving in through our bedroom window. For a week of fine weather they flew in and out all day twittering with pleasure at having found such a home for the summer. At night they roosted in the bedroom, one at each end of the curtain rod, always the male at his chosen end, the female at hers. Seeing us switch on the light and get into bed never worried them, though sometimes they woke and looked down at us for a second or two. At dawn it was always the male that stirred first, sang and then flew out. It was half an hour or more before his mate woke up and then not till he had brought her a beakful of flies which she accepted with much fluttering and twittering. But this idyll could not go on. Our bedroom window faces south-west and often we have to shut it against floods of rain off the sea. With great reluctance, when the weather turned rough, we shut out our swallows and a few days later they built in the outside lavatory (which put that useful building out of bounds for the rest of the summer). To get into this Ty bach (Little House) the swallows had only a four-inch gap at the top of the door. It was staggering to see them come hurtling round the corner of the building on a sharp curve and vanish through that narrow slot without any apparent loss of speed.

That was a kind year for our swallows. They reared two broods and so did several other pairs. By mid August the air above the garden was full of swallows every hour of the day. Often the sparrowhawks came gliding in silence from the oakwood where they had four or five large young to feed. They had no need of quick pursuit or sudden swoop to take the young swallows. Hearing the 'shrik-shrik' of the adults' alarm notes we would look up and see a hawk come quite slowly alongside its victim, take it almost gently and fly off with it. It was terrible to see our swallows going like this. But that is life. And we must accept it as the swallows do. The hawk arrives. There is a moment of terror, pain and death. Then the hawk is gone and once more the swallows are swooping and twittering in the blueness of the sky. Swallows prey on insects and this seems to us good and natural. But when hawks take swallows we are shocked. Yet where is the difference?

Not everyone is as enthusiastic about swallows as we are. Some bee-keepers, for instance, will tell you how many bees a pair of swallows may kill in a season. But bee-keeping is as bedevilled as gardening is by traditional terrors about pests. All the old bee books devoted a horrific chapter to the enemies of the bee. I have one before me now showing a plate with drawings of two dozen creatures which, it is claimed, the bee-keeper should regard with misgiving. They include swallow, great tit, blue tit, red-backed shrike, snail, slug, frog, toad, hedgehog, wood mice and that one-time dread of all bee-keepers, the death's-head hawkmoth! Of the shrike the writer says: 'It will frequently locate its nest near occupied beehives and then it practically lives on the inmates. The only preventive measure is shooting.' The death's-head hawkmoth 'may enter the home of the bee to steal honey. In doing so it frightens the bees thus causing injury by the excitement engendered.' I wonder who invented that myth and how long ago? As for frogs and toads: 'On account of the unobtrusive character of these reptiles, few bee-keepers realize the toll they take from the honey-bee community.'

I have been a bee-keeper for twenty or more years but not for the honey they produce. (Our local woodlands, peat bogs and saltmarshes are poor producers of nectar-bearing flowers.) We keep bees because we like to see them about the garden, busy at the flowers and filling the baskets on their legs with pollen of various colours: bright orange from the mulleins, yellow-green from hazel, dark purple from poppies, pale yellow from willow and apple, dark green from sycamore and so on. Any flower is beautiful. But a flower with a bee or some other insect at work in it is a flower with an added dimension, a doorway leading us into the intricate wonders of pollination. Of course birds and other creatures take our bees. I have watched great tits and great spotted woodpeckers standing on the hives' alighting boards and collecting bees as they arrive and depart. I have no doubt that many other bees are taken in the air by swallows and flycatchers. But I am sure that the total predation is always negligible. Bee numbers are huge and heavy losses are allowed for in the bees' economy. The bee-keeper's real worries should be foul brood and other plagues. He can forget the birds altogether. Even woodpeckers and the dreaded shrike. Even bee-eaters.

In growing flowers for the bees we attract many butterflies also. Polyanthuses, lungwort, *Daphne cneorum*, rock roses, Spanish gorse, aubretia, and early rose species—these are the special delights of the green-veined whites, peacocks, small tortoiseshells, orange tips and brimstones of spring. For the speckled wood our garden has evidently become a forest glade where shade and sunlight are mixed in the right proportions. Chief lures for summer's butterflies are sedums, buddleia, hardy plumbago and caryopteris; and plants of the labiate kind—rosemary, marjoram, sages, mints, lavenders, salvias, thyme, hyssop, cat-mint and bugle. To their colourful and fragrant flowers come meadow brown, gatekeeper, wall, common blue, small copper, later broods of peacock and tortoiseshell and, in a migration year, red admirals and painted ladies. One butterfly, the grayling, visits the garden not for flowers, which it usually ignores, but for warmth and shelter. We see it sunbathing on rocks and walls but if we go near it is quickly up and away for it does not tolerate man as the sippers of nectar often will. Even more remote are the little purple hairstreaks that are common in the oak tops (you need binoculars to see them); totally satisfied by the honeydew they find on high-level leaves they hardly ever make the few yards descent that would bring them into the garden. Day-flying moths such as the silver-y come in late-summer multitudes to the most alluring flowers, to none more so than to those of our strawberry trees (*Arbutus unedo*) from which we sometimes disturb them in clouds as we brush past. Another, much-scarcer day migrant, the humming-bird hawkmoth is also a tippler at many flowers of the garden, even disappearing recklessly into the blue trumpets of *Gentiana sino-ornata*. Nocturnal hawkmoths we attract with white tobacco flowers (*Nicotiana affinis*) that fill the darkness for yards around with perfume. Most are eyed hawks and poplar hawks but once we saw, in the light of a window above, a big, grey, whirring convolvulus hawkmoth.

It chanced, soon after we moved to Ynys Edwin, that the British Trust for Ornithology successfully launched the nation's bird-watchers on a fascinating and valuable activity—a census of common birds. It was a scheme that resulted from the mass destruction of birds by agricultural chemicals in the early sixties. There was a well-fought engagement by conservationists, the first effect of which was a ban on the use in spring of poisonous seed-dressings. (Though even after that an official booklet *Chemicals for the Gardener* advised, very ill advisedly, that those deadly and persistent chemicals, aldrin, dieldrin and heptachlor, were not harmful to wildlife when used as garden pesticides!) A discovery that conservationists made very early in their campaign was how lacking in hard facts they were about bird numbers, embarrassingly so when it came to giving evidence at official inquiries. It was therefore resolved that the bird-watching world must never again be caught napping. And ever since then the commoner breeding birds of Britain have been counted in sample areas and their population fluctuations sensitively measured.

Inspired by this project I took myself off round the fields and woods of Ynys-hir to census the breeding birds. Following techniques recommended by the B.T.O. I mapped the stations of singing males and tried to determine the size of some of their territories. This was fairly straightforward with most thrushes, warblers, wagtails, finches, flycatchers, tits and nuthatches; very difficult with woodpigeons, jays, owls, ducks and woodcock. But I ended up with what I think were fairly good population statistics. One thing was clear: the wealth of birds in some habitats was in vivid contrast with their poverty in others. This census I have kept up over the years; and as Ynys Edwin is included in the survey area it has been interesting to see how our garden, increasingly furnished with ground cover, shrubs, saplings, hedges and climbers, has become a much more favoured breeding habitat for small woodland birds than the near-by woods which, because of years of intensive grazing by sheep, have lost nearly all their undergrowth.

Gardening for the Birds

In making our half-acre garden we have learnt this at least: that there is more to attracting birds than having a bird-table and planting cotoneasters. (Indeed, though we cherish our many cotoneasters for their beauty we must admit that they have not been the success with the birds that we hoped for. We intended them for the winter waxwings but most of the berries on ours are wolfed by blackbirds early in the fall and the only waxwings that have ever come near us, one snowy January, had to make do with hawthorn berries in field hedges.) We have tried in a modest way to be as ecological as we could, creating as natural a mosaic of habitats as possible even though using mostly non-native plants. We have kept in mind that it truly was a garden we wanted and not the sort of wild thicket that a garden, especially a shrub garden, can so easily become if you let it go. We have arrived, we hope, at a reasonable compromise: a garden that is fairly under control but which has a tangible air of the wilderness.

ໄ➤ 11. Birth of a Bird Reserve

The years have gone since Penny and I came to live at Ynys Edwin and there have been many changes, especially after the death in 1966 of Hubert Mappin who had owned Ynys-hir estate (which includes Ynys Edwin) since 1929. He was a retiring, gentle, kindly man in whose hands Ynys-hir with its woodlands, marshes and estuary had retained a tranquillity and wild beauty now rare in a countryside steadily being degraded by conspicuous chalet parks, ill-concealed caravan sites and by houses and other buildings out of character in rural Wales.

Hubert Mappin loved gardens, trees and the world of nature. And honey bees. Many a summer's day I saw him with bees all round him as he bent over an open hive, sometimes wearing no protective veil, his arms and hands quite bare, mumbling to the bees as all truly bee-mad people do. ('Bee-mad' is not derogatory —it describes those rare souls who handle bees by instinct and seem to enjoy mysterious affinities with them.) You will not be surprised to hear that such a man as Hubert Mappin had little use for blood sports. I daresay in his younger days he had done some shooting (this was almost inevitable with his country gentleman upbringing) but by the time we knew him he had long outgrown all that. By then he was keeping Ynys-hir virtually as a private nature reserve (as far as this was compatible with farming) and I remember him angrily turning the otter hunt off his stream. It was because he knew that Penny and I shared many of his views about the countryside that he invited us to live at Ynys Edwin. And for seven years before he died I often helped him to warden his domain by turning back wildfowlers who came trespassing across to the estuary.

His death was the start of an anxious period. What would now happen to Ynys-hir? We had two thoughts to give us some comfort. We knew that his widow, Patricia, wanted if at all possible to keep the estate just as he had made it, retaining its quiet beauty and its status as a wildlife refuge. Further, we were consoled by the knowledge that with his dying hand he had signed a covenant empowering the National Trust to safeguard the place against the worst forms of commercial exploitation. At least that would prevent Ynys-hir, if it had to be sold, from falling into the hands of developers and speculators, the smartest of whom had immediately begun to make inquiries. Come what may, the oakwoods would not be felled and replaced by conifers, which is what happens on so many estates that fall into the hands of financiers. Nor would the fields be covered with caravans or chalets.

The decision came at last: the estate was to be sold. But it would go if possible to someone sympathetic to conservation. But who? Ideally all estates that are natural wildlife refuges should pass into the hands of wildlife trusts. I am thinking especially of low-fertility areas whose reclamation for agriculture is highly expensive and then produces only third-rate land on which vast amounts of fertilizer must be squandered for evermore. Cors Fochno, the peat bog behind Borth, is an example of such an area. Its centre is a National Nature Reserve whose value as a wildlife habitat depends on the drainage being almost nil. Yet round its margins men and machines are always trying to wring the water out of this great acid sponge that would be far better left as a haven for sundews, the large heath butterfly and the geese that graze there in winter. A modern Welsh historian has written that the draining of the marshes of Malltraeth, Porthmadog and Cors Fochno was 'beneficial to everyone'. But with this learned author I totally disagree.

Too often when wildlife-rich estates come on to the market their value is far beyond the resources of the local naturalists' trust. So it was with Ynys-hir. But, we wondered, what about the Royal Society for the Protection of Birds? Patricia Mappin proved sympathetic to this idea. And in due course the R.S.P.B.'s director, Peter Conder, came from the society's headquarters at Sandy, Bedfordshire. He arrived on a March day of raw east wind. The world was grey and shrivelled; there was no sky; the oakwoods were black and lifeless; a dismal haze hid the estuary and its flocks of wildfowl; and the Dyfi-side hills that should have stood up as a splendid background were lost in the filthiest murk. Not a day we would have chosen to show off the charms of the estate. I took Peter round, trying to make up for the gloom and absence of birds by giving him a word-picture of what Ynys-hir is like on better days.

As we got near their clump of Scots pines our pair of ravens rose and circled impressively, proudly trumpeting their owner-ship of the site, for after eight years they were still using their old nest. We watched them as they flew across the sky at speed to chivvy off a buzzard that had floated too near. Beyond the pines, as we walked along the ridge of Ynys Feurig, a lovely pale hen harrier sailed closely past. And, final touch, when we went to look at the heronry, there was a peregrine perched on one of the herons' tallest pines. Maybe these fine raptors helped the cause. For despite the east wind and the gloom, Peter Conder had no difficulty in seeing the possibilities of the place and went away full of enthusiasm. To buy Ynys-hir the R.S.P.B. successfully launched an appeal, an important contribution coming from the West Wales Naturalists' Trust.

So most of Ynys-hir estate became an R.S.P.B. reserve. A blow had been struck for conservation and by coincidence another occur-red at about the same time: the neighbouring Dyfi estuary was declared a National Nature Reserve by the Nature Conservancy. This means that although, in deference to long tradition, wild-fowling is still permitted in the wide, seaward end of the estuary, the narrower head of the estuary adjoining Ynys-hir estate has become a refuge where wildfowl are fully protected. So two sanctuaries exist in mutual support, an arrangement that suits all concerned. The conservationist, though perhaps unable to under-stand why people want to go shooting, is happy that they can't shoot everywhere. The wildfowler is contented because he appreciates that refuge areas are essential to the future of wildfowl stocks. He also knows well enough that every evening plenty of duck will quit the refuge to go off and feed in the surrounding countryside. To get there they have to fly over the guns that lie in wait. It's the same at dawn; the wildfowlers are there again,

awaiting the return flight. Men who gladly leave their warm beds
to go and lie in a mud-hole in the darkness of a winter estuary
amid snow and east winds in the hope of getting a shot at a duck,
such men are clearly possessed by some extraordinarily powerful
and primitive urge. I am torn between admiration of their hardi-
ness and despair that they feel it necessary to destroy what is so
beautiful and innocent. If they always killed cleanly I might more
easily accept it. But, shooting in near darkness, they cannot see to
recover all they cripple. (Many have no dog with them.) It is left
for those of us who come along the estuary in daylight to pick up
here a duck and there a wader scuttling wretchedly along a creek
with a broken wing. There are also the many victims who fly on,
carrying in their flesh lead pellets that may well bring gangrene
and slow death.

What, I wonder, is your attitude to words like 'reserve' and
'sanctuary'? 'Bird sanctuary', though still in popular use, has long
been out of favour among conservationists, especially those who
like to think of themselves as scientific. I was once at a conservationists' meeting that almost unanimously rejected the word
'sanctuary' on the grounds that it was 'emotional'. But I believe
there is not nearly enough emotion in the conservation movement.
Certainly we need all the science we can get. But we need to have
feelings as well. So to my taste 'reserve' is chilly and uninspiring
and is far too much like 'preserve' which suggests pheasants and
guns and gamekeepers' gibbets. I prefer 'sanctuary' which implies
genuine respect for wildlife. But call a place what you will,
reserve or sanctuary, it still needs defining for the naïve sort of
visitors (mercifully they are few) who, having arrived at Ynys-hir
reserve look round with genuine puzzlement at the wild scene, all
this woodland, marsh and estuary where the birds are just as keen
on not being watched as they are in most other places. I think
what they expect, these people, is that as soon as they come through
the gate they will see tame and amicable birds advancing from all
sides with greetings, songs and general goodwill. They seem
quite surprised when they look across the saltings and see two
thousand ducks and not one with its wings clipped and eating
corn from a bucket. This is an inevitable way of thinking in a

world increasingly littered with wildfowl collections, country zoos and safari parks.

But people can learn. Some of them, after all, have never really seen wild birds before. In a way they know that such creatures exist because they've seen them on television. But I suspect they keep them in a special place as part of their television dream world and don't relate them to the living world at all. Even when you take them into a hide on the estuary and show them wild ducks and waders at a few yards range they see them framed in a viewing slot that has something in common with a television screen. The scene is still not quite real for them. So they poke an arm at full length through the slot to point out a bird and are disappointed when the bird flies off in alarm. The birds on the telly behave themselves better than that. But most reserve visitors are quite sophisticated. They know that a wild bird can both see and hear acutely and they enter a hide as it should be entered—with the respect with which they would go into a church.

I can imagine a few, a very few, of my readers getting increasingly impatient at this point. These are the anti-reserve-visiting school. Why, they demand to know, why allow people to come to reserves at all? If you create a bird reserve, they say, then it should be what it claims to be, a place truly reserved for birds to enjoy in peace and not to be gawped at by people. So, they would argue, an estate like Ynys-hir was better as it used to be—private, secluded, a genuine bird sanctuary where people seldom intruded. Undoubtedly there is some merit in this argument. But realities have to be faced. How much public support would there be for wildlife refuges if people were never allowed to visit them? And the fortunate truth is that, provided reserve visiting is arranged on sensitive lines, then many people can enter and see yet not intrude. Miracles can be worked with hides and screened approaches and a little education on how to behave. There is the additional safeguard that in a properly run reserve only about a third of it need be frequented by visitors and then only on carefully selected trails. Another third should be visited only by the warden and his helpers. And the last third should hardly ever be visited by anybody. So perhaps the name 'sanctuary' could be retained for this specially reserved area.

When I have explained to people who are new to the idea that a bird reserve is not a zoo but a place where wildness is everything, then I often see their minds swing to the other extreme. They immediately assume that all that needs to be done in a bird reserve is to make a few hides with trails to them and then sit back and let nature play. So I find myself giving a lecture on reserve management. I have to explain why it is that a nature reserve, far from being left to nature, can be a place where man intervenes quite often. A bird-reserve warden looks at his pools, his marshes, his woods, his hillsides and sees that they are changing all the time, that the vegetation is always on the move and that some species, if there is nothing to check their growth, are sure to be elbowing out others. This may be good or it may be bad for those birds particularly in need of protection. So crucial decisions must be made. The warden has to determine at what stage he must try to hold the vegetation in suspension. In order to check a reed bed that is invading a pool, or brambles rollicking through a wood, or gorse prancing across a field, he and his helpers go to work with bill-hook and scythe and so take on a job that will need to be repeated year after year.

To illustrate these problems of vegetation control I have taken people through the woods at Ynys-hir and told them how the oak is under ferocious attack by the sycamore. They look up at the trees, oak and sycamore growing so quietly together some halcyon morning, and clearly they find it hard to accept the reality behind the idyll: that the trees are engaged in a long and desperate struggle that will end only when one or the other falls away in disease and death. Their roots fight underground for the soil's nutrients. Their leaves compete for light. And in high winds their branches lash at each other as if in anger. Then I explain that, for various reasons, the alien sycamore is spreading far more rapidly than the native oak and, if permitted, must ultimately turn our oakwood into a predominantly sycamore wood. 'But what's wrong with that?' visitors have asked. I have then tried to explain why most conservationists are unenthusiastic about the sycamore. Admitted it is a handsome sturdy tree, good for wind shelter, and that in April it roars with bees from dawn to deep dusk, so eager are they for its nectar. But against it are grave accusations. Except in its brief flowering time it is a poor tree for insects: very few caterpillars eat the leaves of sycamore compared with the multitudes that grow fat on the leaves of oaks every June just when countless small woodland birds need lavish supplies on which to feed their young. And there is also the disadvantage that sycamore casts so deep a shade that hardly any shrub survives below it; and a woodland bird reserve needs a wealth of under-storey shrubs for birds to nest in.

Sometimes as I speak of these things a grey squirrel comes rippling along the trail. My visitors understand about grey squirrels and how they have 'driven out the red squirrel' (the expression is always the same). I am therefore able to make the parallel: just as an alien squirrel ousts a native squirrel, so an alien tree (the sycamore was introduced from south Europe) threatens a native tree. Not that I am entirely anti-sycamore. Every kind of tree adds variety to the woods and, after all, we do see birds feeding in sycamores at times. So I hope that Ynys-hir will keep some of its biggest sycamores even though they scatter their winged seeds far through the wood. Once on the ground they are not eaten as avidly as acorns are by birds and animals. And when they germinate, the young sycamores are better able to survive in the woodland shade than are infant oaks. Hence their success in life.

One of the splendours of Ynys-hir is the oakwood called Coed Penrhyn (Wood along the Ridge). It clothes the rocky spine that is the reserve's central feature and which looks north across former wetlands to the estuary. It is barely a mile long, this wood, but even so is one of the largest surviving fragments of the medieval Boskus de Lissecoed I spoke of in Chapter 1. As such it is precious. And it owes its survival to the devotion of a long line of owners and especially to Hubert Mappin who held on to Coed Penrhyn when it had become fashionable (the fashion continues) to clear away oakwoods and replace them by conifers. For he was well aware that an oakwood is richer in wildlife than any other land habitat and that in keeping his oaks he was providing a sanctuary for birds and mammals, not to mention myriads of smaller creatures that depend on oak leaves, oak bark, oak wood or acorns for their livelihood.

I have often taken R.S.P.B. members down the woodside to the stile at the bottom where, clear of the trees, the view is across the marsh to Ynys Edwin. Perhaps the month is May, the morning delicious and the gnats and horseflies of summer not yet thought of. Everywhere there is birdsong because birds are more numerous along the bushy edge of a wood than within the shade of the trees. Willow warblers, pied flycatchers, blackcaps, thrushes, tree pipits, wood warblers, redstarts, garden warblers, blackbirds, nut-hatches, woodpeckers—all in their special idioms add beauty to the hour. From the oaks of Coed Penrhyn we venture into the quaking peat bog to see the flowers peculiar to wet places: strange insect-eating sundews of three species, the great sundew (in its greatness it towers up to no more than a few inches) being the most attractive of the trio; bog rosemary creeping shyly among the sphagnum mosses; asphodel, its leaves only tiny green swords so early in the season; heath spotted orchids almost thinking of flowering; attractive rushes, sedges and stately grasses. My visitors are delighted by it all. Simply walking a few yards across a bog—something they had never dared do before—has opened their eyes to new wonders. Till now a bog has been no more to them than a squalid, dangerous mire that ought to be drained. But now it has become a world of delight.

On the peat bog I have also pointed out to visitors the menace of the rhododendrons that stand all round like a wall. But no, a wall suggests something stationary; and the rhododendrons of Ynys Edwin bog move ever forwards like a dark green tide as their seedlings spring up before them in the sphagnum moss. If we did not have willing hands to help us fight back this threat we would soon lose the entire marsh under the sort of jungle that had invaded the adjacent Scots pinewood, most of which no one had been able to get into for the past twenty years, so total was the interlacing of the long, tough, curving branches of the rhododen-drons. If only rhododendron were rich in birds! If even one rare species found a refuge in those dark shadows, how we would treasure these thickets—the product of a century's growth. But the bleak truth is that very little bird life ever stirs in all that dense cover except when in some winters we get a vast invasion of roosting starlings.

It was Sir Uvedale Price of Hereford and other landowners who in the late eighteenth century succeeded in popularizing in Britain this *Rhododendron ponticum* that we now aspire to eliminate almost entirely from our Ynys-hir woodlands so that sunlight can enter and encourage less stifling, more bird-full trees to spring up instead. But we must not think too harshly of Sir Uvedale and his fellows. They were gardeners with undying enthusiasm for picturesque landscapes; and a few rhododendrons clumped tastefully here and there no doubt helped their design. The mischief came after them in the nineteenth century when the pheasant-rearing craze really began to scourge the British countryside and landowners planted rhododendrons all through their woods as shelter for their pheasants in winter.

Contrary to what some may suppose, the life of a bird-reserve warden is far from being that of a solitary stroller through wood and marsh, communing with nature like a Romantic poet. Truly a warden needs to love his fellow men, for people are visiting reserves in ever-increasing numbers. Most come simply to see and learn about birds. But there is another quite numerous group (without whom life for me would be impossible) who come to help. In all weathers and at all seasons they arrive at Ynys-hir, at their own expense, to give their time and energy with unfailing cheerfulness. I have had marvellous aid from young and old— voluntary wardens who stay a week or several weeks; school groups who come partly to help and partly to pursue field studies; the Young Ornithologists' Club; the Conservation Corps; students from the University of Wales; scouts and guides both British and foreign; R.S.P.B. groups; local residents sympathetic to the cause; Outward Bound and adventure school parties, both civilian and from the services. One of their main tasks is the clearing of the rhododendrons which, when we began work, covered about fifty acres. For me this flow of practical aid is one of the most cheering faces of modern society. And when I see

N

these volunteers all working happily at their tasks, I wonder how many more people would be willing to give a hand in the countless conservation schemes that are in progress all over the country if only they knew how much their help would be appreciated.

Life for the warden and his helpers at Ynys-hir is far from being entirely taken up with swiping at sycamores or being nasty to rhododendrons. There is scope for more direct forms of creativity. Trees to be planted, for instance. We are growing alders for siskins that will come for seeds in winter; Scots pines at the heronry to replace in years to come the tall trees the birds breed in at present. And we are adding to the birches, hazels, hollies and hawthorns that are already here. As a monument to optimism we have even put in hornbeams for the hawfinch, though that desirable bird is entirely absent from the district. (Bird-watchers of the twenty-first century ticking hawfinch off on your lists as you stand under the great hornbeams of Ynys-hir, we send you greetings!)

In the woods we have also provided nest-boxes. I suppose there are a few ecological purists who would sniff at all our nest-boxes as quite unnatural. And certainly they have had their effect on our bird population—a noteworthy increase in pied flycatchers for instance, no bird being more addicted to boxes. I have often claimed, though I admit I have never actually tried it, that if, in the critical week of the year when boxes are being so fiercely squabbled over, someone were to stand in Coed Penrhyn holding a box up over his head he would soon get a pied flycatcher excitedly popping in and out of it. All right, I'm exaggerating; but I speak truth when I say that the more boxes we put up in our woods the more pied flycatchers come and breed here. So we wonder how many we could attract if we provided 1,000 boxes instead of the present 150? Clearly there must be a limit somewhere but with our fifty pairs of flycatchers I'm sure we are not yet near it for there are several woods and spinneys that have not so far been provided with boxes. Meanwhile I doubt if the artificial increase in pied flycatchers has done anything to upset the ecological balance. True, they compete with other small birds

for food but the oakwood's caterpillar harvest is so generous
every year that there seems more than enough for all. Certainly
the nest-boxes give much pleasure to our human visitors who
come far to see this engaging flycatcher, so confiding and watch-
able, showing off his neat black and white plumage as he sings
enthusiastically among the buds of early May. Then there are the
blue tits, great tits, nuthatches, redstarts and tawny owls that are
all happy to lease our boxes for a season. We should be thankful.
Elsewhere in the world we might not be so fortunate. As when a
friend of mine put up nest-boxes on trees in an African national
park: not a single bird ever went near them! (But will African
birds eventually learn the use of boxes?)

For a wide view of Ynys-hir in its estuary setting under the
shapely line of the Meirionnydd hills you cross the main road and
follow paths through the bracken up the hill called Foel Fawr
where the reserve reaches its highest point. Here among the grey
rocks are the nesting places of wheatear, whinchat, tree pipit and
many a strong-voiced wren; and some nights the purring of
nightjars comes through the mothy darkness. Choicest wildflowers of the hill are the insect-trapping butterworts that in May
hang purple flowers on neatly curved stems. Then in July the
elegant little ivy-leaved bellflowers open pale blue cups half-
hidden in the grass. Summer also brings crimson-purple sheets
of bell heather and swiftly passing dark green fritillary butterflies;
and family parties of ravens playing in the wind over the summit
rocks. The brackeny slopes tilt sharply down through birches and
oaks into the dingle of the hastening Einion that soon drops over
Furnace Falls, then flows on to form a beautiful margin along the
lower levels of the reserve. Here in recent years mergansers have
begun to breed, hiding their nests in the banks. Here, too, are
grey wagtails, dippers and sometimes the flash of blue that is a
kingfisher. Slowing between banks of tidal mud the Einion joins
the Dyfi under the motte called Domen Las (Green Mound) on
which in the twelfth century the defenders of south Wales built a
wooden fort to challenge invaders from the north. Then perhaps
for many centuries after the fort had decayed the mound stood
bare until, I would guess, early in the nineteenth century, some

owner of Ynys-hir thought fit to crown the knoll with Scots pines that stand today. To him we are grateful: for the weather-battered old pines now house the nests of two or three dozen pairs of herons who come and go all day in slow, grave flight. Under the trees in holes in the banks of the mound several pairs of shelducks have their nests. And what birds bring more life and colour to the river bank than shelducks?

Despite being so varied Ynys-hir had long lacked one habitat especially precious to wildlife and that is freshwater pools. There were a few marshy fields and there were often floods in winter: but no permanent open water apart from the river. So into one of the fields a few years ago we brought a mechanical digger and a bull-dozer and, during a summer drought, we gouged out a hollow as dry as a moon crater. But if there was no water visible in this hollow there was plenty just below. It was truly frightening to see the five-ton bulldozer working delicately down through the silt a few inches at a time until it was supported by only a skin of floating, tremulous clay and looked certain to disappear at any moment into deep and watery depths. But at last the job was done, the thunder of machinery died away and the hollow was left to fill slowly in the autumn rains. By the first Christmas it was a real pool with an island in the centre; and wigeon were beginning to visit.

Nature gave us a nod of encouragement while we were making this first pool. When the job was only half done, a pair of oyster-catchers arrived from somewhere and nested on the island, though they did well to recognize it as such since there was not yet a drop of water anywhere. We felt this was a true benison upon our efforts because this was the first time that oyster-catchers had ever been known to breed at Ynys-hir. And it was for just such birds as oystercatchers, ringed plovers and little terns that we had planned this island. They are the special birds of stony beaches; but hardly anywhere along the shore these days can the birds have any peace because people and dogs are there all day and every day throughout spring and summer. So on our island we laid a carpet of plastic bags to stifle the weeds; then on top a layer of pebbles to resemble a beach. It is up to the birds to do the rest. So far, apart from the one pair of oystercatchers, only common sandpipers have nested on our island. But in experiments like this you live by faith.

When spring came we planted sedges, aquatic grasses, pond-weeds and amphibious bistort in the shallows of the pool: all plants that provide waterfowl not only with cover but also food, for their seeds are nutritious. Meanwhile the water, which for long months had been clouded with silt, began to clear and look healthy. Soon we were cheered by the sight of our first water beetles, water snails, pond skaters, water boatmen and dragon-flies. Then, in the mysterious way fish have of finding their way to new waters, three-spined sticklebacks appeared. And it wasn't long before dabchicks came to dive for the sticklebacks. Still, it was not until we saw the first herons and kingfishers that we began to feel our pool had truly arrived. Since then other birds have dropped in one after another; and to date ten species of duck and a dozen waders have been seen at the pool.

Lately a new pool has been excavated near by. But while the first was made oval with one large central island, the second pond has an interesting, five-lobed shape (with several islets) to provide a maximum length of shoreline. As this is a pool expressly aimed at attracting waders, we made it shallow all over in the hope that, come August and September, at the height of the wader migration, it will be partly dry and provide an interesting pattern of wet mud and puddles for ruffs, stints and sandpipers both common and rare. Dreams? We must wait and see.

I admit these pools are only small affairs, a mere 150 yards across, but they are a start, the first steps in the creation of a mosaic of ponds and marshes of differing sizes, shapes and depths that I hope will eventually change the face of some of Ynys-hir's sea-level land. In any project you have to begin somewhere: and in the drainage-mad days in which we live it is good to have reversed the trend however minutely, to have actually ripped up a few drainage pipes and held back a little water from flowing too hastily away. But let me assure any farmer who may have recoiled from this last sentence in horror that most of Ynys-hir's fields are farmed and thoroughly drained. To be drowning some fields and draining others may sound a little odd. But then we live in a time when farming and wildlife-conservation are, we trust, beginning to learn to live together.

Meanwhile at the other end of the reserve we plan wetlands of a different character. These, we hope, will be a chain of lagoons amid reed swamps where water birds, for centuries bereft of nesting places by drainage schemes, will be able to breed once again. We should remember that the bittern, for instance, was once familiar to Welsh country folk as aderyn y bwn ('the booming bird')—sufficient evidence that it nested widely in Wales, for it is only when on its breeding grounds that this strange cousin of the heron draws in his great breaths and then, exhaling with all his might, lets the surrounding marshlands have the benefit of his splendid voice—the farthest carrying bird sound in all nature. The bittern, after a long absence from Britain, returned to nest in East Anglia in 1911. Now it breeds not only in the east but also in the west, in Lancashire and Anglesey. The question is: will this spread continue? And the answer is that it probably will if more wetlands with extensive reed beds can be provided. It is going to be a crucial test for conservation, this problem of creating more wetlands in a world in which lowering the water table has become a national pre-occupation.

As with bitterns so with harriers. They, too, like to nest in reed beds and no doubt once did so in many parts of Wales. The fortunes of harriers have fluctuated in the last few decades especially those of the hen harrier and Montagu's. In the 1950s there were in some years perhaps ten pairs of Montagu's breeding in the coastal counties of Wales. Since when they seem to have almost completely ceased to breed in Wales: which is hardly surprising since they are being increasingly shot for fun on migration during the great autumnal bird slaughter that goes on every year in many south European countries and on the Mediterranean islands. But meanwhile the hen harrier, formerly an extreme rarity, is slowly gaining ground. (The hen harrier winters in Britain and so avoids the hazards of a journey across south Europe.) As we struggle to create our reed beds at Ynys-hir it is inevitable that these beautiful, long-winged raptors float in and out of our thoughts. Someday, maybe, we shall see their exciting courtship flights above our marshes in spring.

The shortage of wetlands and therefore of breeding places for bitterns, bearded tits, harriers, spoonbills, godwits, ruffs, avocets and other desirable birds is only one way in which the British countryside is out of balance. The excess of pheasants in so many places is another symptom of malaise. I am happy not to have known Ynys-hir early this century when its woods were given over to pheasants. I'm sure the buzzards and sparrowhawks didn't survive here long in those days. I can easily picture the nineteenth-century coverts tyrannized by some ruthless gamekeeper; and gibbets hung with putrifying hawks along with rows of white owls, brown owls, stoats, weasels and polecats. How different today. All this spring there has been not a single call of a pheasant to threaten my peace of mind. Instead four pairs of lovely buzzards circled and wailed over the woods. And three pairs of sparrowhawks nested safely. Tawny owls filled the trees with their music. We have frequently seen peregrines, merlins, hen harriers, kites and barn owls. Raptorial mammals have abounded. It is all so very healthy, having such a robust team of predators to keep the pheasant in his place, his proper place as a bird of crake-like secrecy, hiding in reed beds and other dense cover and hardly ever raising his voice in self-advertisement. So different from the half-tame, crowing multitudes that are fussed over by an army of keepers on Britain's shooting estates and are the chief reason why birds of prey, especially the larger sorts, are still rare in most of England. Take the buzzard for example. Buzzards are protected birds, but only on paper. They thrive abundantly in those parts of Wales where pheasant-rearing is little practised; and there is no doubt that these areas produce enough young buzzards to populate the woods of all England in not many years. Probably every autumn there is a liberal dispersal of buzzards eastwards from Wales, youngsters eager to colonize new districts. But what is their fate? It is rarely possible to prove anything. But there is every reason to suspect that gun, trap and poison still do some very dirty work every year in many an English covert. Pheasants there are big business and big business has no conscience. The continuing (but surreptitious) use of the dreadful pole-trap, which ensures a slow death by torture and which has been illegal since 1908, is evidence of this.

Predators kill other birds besides pheasants; which means that Ynys-hir will never raise battalions of wild ducks or go in for rearing geese as our wildfowling neighbours would like us to do. But what we shall achieve, if all goes well, is a varied and healthy community of animals, birds, plants and trees living together with as much balance and harmony as can be hoped for in a small area islanded in a world where wildlife is increasingly on the defensive. As for the people who have to live in that world, more pressingly as time goes on they are going to need the 'tonic of wildness' (I never tire of quoting Thoreau's apt phrase). And I hope that if they come to Ynys-hir reserve they will have a genuine experience of wildness either in the birds they see and hear or in the trees and the wildflowers. Or simply in the place itself which I trust will always retain something of the wilderness quality of former days.

In writing about this one nature reserve I hope I have said something applicable to wider fields. Not every wild place can become a nature sanctuary but everywhere a little can be done to help our native plants and animals. Often it needs only a thought at the right time and a thicket, a short length of hedge, a single bush or a tiny pool can be saved—habitats minute in themselves yet whose preservation is a lifeline perhaps for a thrush, a butterfly or a colony of frogs or toads. At the other end of the scale are the big areas of land and water, maybe whole districts of mountain, moorland, downland, forest, lake or sea coast. Here the problems of nature conservation get involved with other issues—the preservation of landscape beauty, the organization of National Parks, the management of water resources, the agricultural use of land, the future of forestry plantations, the damming of estuaries or the building of power stations.

When you see the storms of controversy that can suddenly rage over a hitherto peaceful stretch of countryside because someone proposes to build an airport, open a mine or create a reservoir then you realize what almost complete chaos there is at the heart of affairs. You see that although there are planning departments everywhere (some of whose officials really do carry a light in a very dark world) the overall picture is one of an ill-controlled free-for-all in which developers and their supporting financiers are always seeking some new field to adventure in. There is not yet any sufficient guiding philosophy of how the countryside should be treated. Perhaps there never will be, never can be. Perhaps the conservationists must always be an impotent minority moaning their little protests as the oil tide blackens the beaches, as the estuaries vanish behind barrages, as the orchid meadows give place to improved grasslands, as the lichens die on the tree trunks through foul air, and as the oaks go crashing to make way for the Sitka spruces. Perhaps we are doomed to struggle on, saving a little patch here as we lose a greater one there, fighting a battle that is already lost. As the world's resources shrink, as human populations grow more and more like a pestilence, are the pressures on us all and on our land likely to get less? If not, what are we to do? These are vast questions which mere individuals are powerless to cope with. And governments, who could achieve something, do as little as they can get away with doing and then vote another few thousand millions to promote the next stage in the sacred cause of economic growth. What they never tell us, because they think only short-term thoughts, is where it is all leading to, this economic growth, in terms of the squandering of natural resources and the blighting of our habitat. We know we are going to have more people, more houses, more cars, more motorways, more aircraft, more airports, more factories, more goods of all sorts, more towns. But in our over-crowded Britain where are they all going to be put? And what hope is there of saving anything of ultimate value to the spirit of man in terms of natural beauty and wildness; or of health and sanity in the real meaning of these words?

The hope, the one hope perhaps, is in a vast increase in public concern for the ecological well-being of the earth. And though up to now the signs of such a revolution are small, they certainly exist. Trickles of thought are approaching each other from many directions and they could flow together at last as a stream with force enough to burst through the accumulated debris of wrong ideas that have landed us in our present mess. Modern man's naïve faith in perpetual economic growth and ever more industrialization is beginning to be shaken. More and more people are realizing that we cannot go on over-exploiting our finite resources for ever and that we've got to put the brakes on somewhere.

But, politicians tell us, without growth we get mass unemployment. They are probably right. And always will be as long as our economy hinges on making motor cars, aeroplanes and power stations; and getting oil and coal and other minerals out of the earth. Yet are these things truly necessary? When I look round I see everywhere enormous works that need doing, works that would really improve the quality of people's lives, works to improve the environment, all sorts of tasks of rehabilitation of people and places that at present are left largely to volunteers. I would say there is positively no need for anyone to be unemployed for centuries to come, there is so much to be done in our towns and cities and throughout the countryside. You will object perhaps that this would be 'unproductive' work and could not be paid for as the economy is run at present. If this is so then clearly we need a new sort of economy. And the sooner the better because as things are the world about us is becoming more and more uninhabitable. Only a completely new social philosophy, based on conservation and a genuine concern for the health of the environment, of man and of the whole world of nature, can give any hope that life in the twenty-first century will be worth living for anybody.

Certainly in any rehabilitation of the countryside I would like to see many more nature reserves. Not just for the sake of conserving wildlife, which is hard-pressed enough, God knows, but for man himself whose plight is far more desperate than that of many animals. Since I have been warden of a bird reserve I have become increasingly interested in the people who come to visit it. They may think me a very queer sort of bird (seeing my aquiline nose they probably class me among the raptors) but I in my turn find some of them totally fascinating. So many of them show signs of stress, in their faces and in their words; and, unconsciously, it is more than wildlife that they look for in a nature reserve. Without realizing it they are seeking, I think, some way back to a simpler, more natural type of living. They seek it instinctively, like salmon ascending a muddy estuary to find sparkling water near the sources of a river. So I am prepared to believe that the greatest beneficiary of nature reserves will prove in due time to be not nature after all, but man.

Index